Mindshare Market Share

How to use thought-leadership selling to win hearts, minds & budgets in the networked age.

Bernard Lunn

© Bernard Lunn, 2014

Table of Contents

Personal Prologue   4

What You Will Learn   12

Sell To Customers Who Are Being Disrupted   23

Sales is Dead, Long Live Partnerships   30

Turn Secret Sauce Into Unfair Advantage   37

How To Define & Lead Your Own Market   43

Find The Moment Of Sales Truth   57

Internet Changes Everything, Including Sales   66

Reduce Customer Acquisition Cost   71

Do The 4-Step Social Media Dance   81

Nudge The Buy Process In Your Direction   85

© Bernard Lunn, 2014

Focus By Imagining the Press Conference	96
Always Be Qualifying – Listen For Screams	103
Closing - Forget Chess & Play Poker	110
Don't Tell Picasso To Paint By Numbers	120
How To Hire The A Team Sales Guys	126
The IQ & EQ Quadrant	131
Use Your Sales Team As Market Sensors	137
Managing Bring Your Own Everything	147
Turn The 80% Average Into 10% Stars	153
Forecasting In A Disruptive World	167
The Sales Capability Maturity Ladder	178
Sell To YOUR Ideal Customer	184

© Bernard Lunn, 2014

Personal Prologue

I am a shy intellectual who became a salesman in order to eat and, along the way, began to enjoy selling.

If you watch Glengarry Glen Ross, you can see a nightmare world of sales managers who are manipulating sales guys who are selling a product that they know is lousy. The scene where one of them is desperate to close a deal in order that he can pay the hospital for his sick daughter is heartbreaking.

That is not the world of sales that I started to eventually enjoy and which I describe in this book. It was however the harsh world that this shy intellectual was thrown into after leaving the dreaming spires of Oxford University in 1977.

These were hard times, like the Great Recession and maybe worse, full of strikes and riots that almost became the second English Civil War – the Sex Pistols and the Clash resonated with this reality. There were no good jobs, so I sold encyclopedias to American soldiers in Germany for 9 months, which was enough to pay off my debts (tiny by today's college debt standards). Then I started looking for "real" work, the type of work that college graduates are supposed to do. The conversations went like this:

- **Me: "I got a 2.1 in History from Oxford"**

- **Employer (stifling a yawn): "Yes, what else have you done?"**

- **Me: "I sold encyclopedias successfully for 9 months"**

- **Employer: "You can sell! Well that is interesting. Let me tell you about what we do..."**

I was typecast. The shy intellectual had become a salesman. Oh well, it paid the bills and, as I loved to ski, my bills were not small. Luckily, I stumbled upon the IT industry and it started to become fun and lucrative.

I went to all the sales training classes where we were taught to CONTROL the sale, by controlling the customer. That was the only way to hit your numbers. I accepted that, because it was what I had learned as an encyclopedia salesman.

The encyclopedia sales pitch was scripted. You literally had to learn it by heart before knocking on doors. Like many others I thought, *"I am not a robot, I am a human selling to humans, I can do better than this"*. I tried winging it - and failed dismally. The script was brilliantly designed to manipulate how people think; it worked.

From simple one-to-one encyclopedia selling, I graduated to persuading large companies to part with a lot of cash. I learned the art of the *complex, big-ticket enterprise sale*.

You can still recognize the world of encyclopedia sales in the training materials for enterprise sales teams. Despite the fact that "the Internet changes everything", we still sell based on the same principles and techniques I learned as an encyclopedia salesman.

> The sales manuals need an update.

When the Internet started to become mainstream around the turn of the century, I decided that I had become like the Polish cavalry at the start of World War Two. I had mastered a game that had changed. The Polish cavalry was renowned for its mastery of riding horses at great speed while also shooting with great accuracy; none of that was much use when the Germans attacked with planes and tanks.

> The Internet changes everything, including sales.

So I chose to work in startups that mastered the skills of the Internet age, such as how to get in the door using search and social media and how to close by converting from a free service to a paid service. Those techniques are now taught at colleges such as Stanford and in the accelerators and incubators of the startup world. Then I noticed that some of the most adept practitioners of those arts were asking me to explain how to create partnerships with companies using the old-fashioned sales techniques that I had mastered Pre-Internet.

That led me to write this book. I realized that these were two different worlds and "never the twain shall meet". The Polish cavalry analogy did not tell the whole story. The born-digital generation wanted to learn the Pre-Internet sales skills, but they wanted them updated for the Internet age. At the other end of the demographics, those who had mastered the complex, big-ticket enterprise sale needed to be able to incorporate the modern Internet tools and techniques in a meaningful and practical way.

Selling is a human business. You are one human trying to convince another human. The encyclopedia sale took about 90 minutes, of which the first 15-20 minutes was just conversation to get acquainted. You could see the moment of truth when a couple (it was almost always a married couple with young children) became convinced (or not); you could see it in their eyes. It took me a while to realize that even a 6 month complex, big-ticket enterprise sale with multiple stakeholders came down to that same "moment of truth". You have to win hearts and minds. All sales are emotional sales. We rationalize the decision in numbers, because that is how we keep score in business, but humans make decisions with their heart. You have to win the hearts before you get a chance to win the mind. That is obvious in an encyclopedia sale, which is all about the dreams and aspirations that parents have for their children. It is less obvious in an enterprise sale, which is why this book goes beyond the obvious "reading body language" to focus on the emotional key to a sale.

You have to win hearts *and* minds; both have to be aligned. Selling big-ticket deals to big, complex enterprises during times of disruptive change requires a lot of intelligence. To convince the CXO level of a Global 2000 firm, you need to have a deep understanding of technology *and* business *and* the market that the customer operates in *and* how the world is changing. That is not a job for shallow smooth talking people; you need thought-leadership selling.

> You need the magic quadrant of high EQ and high IQ to win over both hearts and minds.

When the key decision-maker or influencer becomes convinced in their heart and in their mind, you will see it in their eyes. This is the enterprise sales moment of truth. This may come 3 month into a sale and you may have 3 months more to get to contract and you may have many more people to align, but from this moment on the sale is "yours to win or lose".

Your path to market-share is through these moments of truth.

> First you get mindshare and then you get market-share.

Of course a complex, big-ticket enterprise sale is – more complex. It is more complex because you have an organizational entity to convince. This is where enterprise sales classes taught us about management hierarchies, decision-making units and budgets. However the sale still comes down to individuals and what makes them tick. In the Internet age, these individuals are connected through networks that cross the traditional management hierarchies and often cross the organizational boundary. The key influencer may well be outside the payroll of the company that you are selling to. "Wirearchies" are replacing hierarchies.

What You Will Learn

I wrote this book for busy people who are building a business. You don't have time for a PHD dissertation on sales. Our attention spans have become shorter thanks to the Internet. I have made the chapter titles self-explanatory, so that you can dip in and out, if you prefer that to reading sequentially.

> Speed-readers and skimmers are welcome.

You will get value from this book if one of these descriptions fits you:

1. **Technical founder of an Internet startup.** Technical founders are mostly "consciously competent" in development (good and always figuring out how to get better), but need just enough knowledge to be "consciously incompetent" in Sales and Marketing (know what you don't know, so that you can hire well). In the early days of a new venture, you may have to do some of this yourself.

Later you will need to hire and manage people to do this; it is useful to understand what the people who you are hiring will be doing.

2. **Head of digital marketing.** The relationship between sales and marketing has always been complex, but it is getting more complex as the Internet changes the rules once again. You are deeply versed in the digital "growth hacking" techniques such as SEO, SEM, Viral Networking, A/B Testing, Content Marketing and Freemium. You have engineered a perfect quantitative feedback loop between the product and marketing; everything is recorded with scientific precision in your Marketing Automation system. You now need to make sure that you are not blind-sided by what users are *really* thinking, but not revealing by their actions online; these are thoughts that they might reveal to another human. You need to create an analog qualitative feedback loop to augment your digital quantitative feedback loop by using sales people as "market sensors".

3. **Veteran sales manager.** You need to save those on your team who are trapped in "unconscious competence". These are the sales executives who have been the stars of the old control oriented Pre-Internet school of selling. They are so good at the game that they can "do it in their sleep". These are the guys who always "hit the numbers" – until suddenly they find themselves drifting down from the A Team to the B Team because the game that they had mastered has changed.

4. **Young outside sales person.** The modern equivalent of the door-to-door salesman is the "inside sales" person working the phones. Some of you may want to get out of sales as quickly as possible; you may be studying software engineering at night. Others want to get into "real sales" where you meet people face to face and get the big deals; this book is for you.

5. **Head Of Inside Sales.** You sit at the

interface between Digital Marketing and Outside Sales. You want to identify those "natural sales people" who are itching to get out into the field to get the bigger deals and then help them to transition properly. This is not a simple transition and it is a totally different career path from going into management.

> Sales is back in focus because Enterprise Software is back in fashion.

Google, Facebook and Twitter sucked the air out of the indirect, ad-driven consumer model. Therefore, many entrepreneurs wisely switched their attention to a direct revenue model, by focusing on the cash-hoards that are currently at record levels in big companies.

Business Week has commented on the increased focus on sales:

"In the past few years the number of sales programs at colleges and universities in the U.S. has exploded, according to the "Sales Education Program Landscape Study" done by the Center for Sales Leadership, run out of DePaul University's College of Commerce. In 2007, courses in sales were offered at 44 U.S. schools, a number that jumped to 101 schools in 2011. Now 32 schools offer a major, minor, or concentration in sales, up from nine just four years ago, the study found. Even MBA programs are starting to get into the game, with 15 now including sales courses as part of their graduate programs in 2011 and six offering an MBA with a sales concentration."

Some technically oriented founders would prefer to "write sales out of the script" by automating the whole process of revenue generation. Hope is not a strategy. The hope that your product is "so amazing that it will sell itself", usually gets dashed against these three rocks of reality:

1. **Nobody cares about your startup.** It is one thing for a big company to launch an amazing product. Most startups that launch amazing products get ignored. Obscurity is your biggest enemy and old-fashioned human hustle is the best antidote to obscurity. That is why the founders of Airbnb sold to the first apartment owners door to door in New York City; they "did things that don't scale".

2. **You are competing for scarce attention online.** All those digital marketing techniques, taught in so many accelerator classes, are leading to digital fatigue. Many savvy digital marketers are aware of this and sell their own services using old-fashioned tools, such as billboards, telephones, conferences and face-to-face meetings.

One simple observation is that many influential people are easier to reach by phone than by email; they welcome a break from email.

3. **Channels augment success but don't create success.** You may think, "I don't want to hire a sales team, I want to sell through channels". That may be right for you, but recognize that channels won't take you seriously until you have proven the proposition by selling some customers yourself.

There are four growth inflection points where Mindshare to Marketshare will be most valuable:

1. **When you first create a repeatable sales process.** You need to replace the passion and creativity of the founders that got the early customers with a repeatable, scalable sales process. Too much process too soon is as damaging as too little too late; getting the balance right is hard.

2. **When your market goes into hyper-growth.** The good news is that

customers now understand the need for your "ahead-of-its-time" solution. The bad news is that this is the time when lots of competitors flood in. You can deride these competitors as copycats, but unless you scale fast, your company will become a footnote in history. This is tough, because you have to scale without losing what made you special in the early days.

3. **When you hit a speed bump.** When the numbers don't look so good, you need to assess whether you have a tactical or a strategic issue. If you assess it as merely a tactical issue, you just need to execute better and this will include re-vitalizing sales and marketing. Or, the speed bump may be signaling a fundamental market shift that requires a strategic re-evaluation (disruption can sneak up on you).

4. **When you are expanding into new geographies.** You need scalable processes without making the cultural mistakes that kill your market entry.

5. **When you are expanding into adjacent markets.** This is like geographic expansion where you need to get the balance right between adapting to unique needs and having a scalable process.

This book is divided into three sections:

1. **Strategy**. In the Before Internet world, strategy preceded sales in an assembly line step-by-step model[1]. You created a strategy, then you built a product, finally you hired a sales team to sell the product. In the After Internet world, we have to move to a more agile model where we get constant feedback loops from the market and this feedback informs company strategy and influences the product. In this emerging reality, sales people are not just "pitching machines"; they are your market sensors. That requires a new breed of sales people and new way to manage them. It also requires a new

---

[1] For software developers, the analogy is the waterfall method.

© Bernard Lunn, 2014

way to think about strategy.

2. **Thought-Leadership Selling**. These chapters describe the key stages of the business sales process, which is like a game of chess:

- **Beginning**. This is how you get leads. Your Pawn to King Four opening move won't win you the game, but a dumb move will probably lose you the game.

- **Middle**. This is how you prove that your product fits your customer's need. Yes, this phase is mind-numbingly complex. Some players just have an "eye for the board". The rest of us have to think it through.

- **End**. This is how you close the contract and get the cash (and check-mate the King).

3. **Managing in this new reality**. The Internet has changed how sales and marketing works. The Internet has disrupted the companies that we are

selling to. With all this change, how do we manage in order to build a business with scalable and repeatable processes? The closing chapters deal with management issues, such as aligning sales and marketing, hiring and firing, technology support for sales productivity, coaching and forecasting.

Sell To Customers Who Are Being Disrupted

The Internet fundamentally erodes the competitive advantage that large companies built during the 20th Century and also creates massive new digital-first opportunities.

The globalization wave is hitting at the same time as the digitization wave and they are connected because "bits don't stop at borders". The rise of the "Rest[2]" means that we can no longer assume that, if it works in America or Europe, then the rest of the world will fall into place. Big western firms now have massive new markets to move into, but they also have to worry that some previously unknown competitor from the Rest will invade their home market (like Amazon meets Alibaba, Cisco meets Huawei and Apple meets Xiaomi).

---

[2] The Rest means countries "formerly known as emerging", or more simply, countries other than America, Europe and Japan.

© Bernard Lunn, 2014

These two tsunamis of change are crashing down on the companies that you are selling to. You do not want to be the waiter at the hotel asking the guest if she wants another cocktail just when the tsunami is hitting the beach. *You must be relevant to what the CXO level guys are thinking:*

- You do *not* want to be selling systems to make bank tellers more productive to a Bank that is trying to decide how many branches to close and how to sell to the 70% of the world that is unbanked by using mobile money services.

- You do *not* want to be selling a new enrollment system to a college that is trying to decide out how to cut costs radically in order to prosper in a world where most people get educated through online classes.

- You do *not* want to be selling retail Point of Sales systems to a Retailer while their Board is figuring how to not be "showroomed" to death by customers who look offline but buy online.

> It is not easy to figure out "where the puck is moving to[3]" in your market. It is hard, but if you do not know this, then you are flying blind in a hurricane.

This disruption creates a new challenge for your sales team. The CXO level executives at your prospects know very well that their world is changing and that they cannot simply keep doing what worked so well in the past. At the same time they have to keep the current numbers looking good, so they present a public face of *"it's business as usual"*. That message is meant for investors, customers and partners.

---

[3] Quote from Wayne Gretzky, the ice hockey star, popularized in business by Scott McNealey, CEO of Sun Microsystems.

© Bernard Lunn, 2014

The "it's business as usual" message is also meant for their own middle management. The CXO level executives need middle managers to "keep their eye on the ball", so that they keep making the quarterly numbers with the same products and services that worked in the past.

This is what creates the problem for your sales guys. They will be in mid sales campaign, working with middle management executives at the customer that are quite sincerely interested in the solution presented by your sales team. In the version of reality that your customers *publicly* proclaim, your solution is perfectly aligned to their needs. Publicly, "it's business as usual" and so you sell "as usual". Your team is doing all the right qualification process steps, such as checking budgets and timescales.

Then suddenly, your sales guy wakes up and sees an announcement. The business unit that she is selling to has been sold, declared non-core or some other message that says that it is "game over". Your sales person calls the customer and basically asks:

"WTF?"

The customer, who is in the dark, says something like:

> "I really don't know. There is an internal announcement in 10 minutes, I should know more then".

30 minutes later, the manager at your prospective customer calls your sales person and asks for a job. Your sales person knows that her own quarter is blown and will have guessed that, if this customer is taking this strategy, then other customers will soon follow suit; so she is nervous about her own job. So the soon to be ex customer and worried sales person arrange to meet for a drink or coffee to commiserate.

To avoid this fate, you need to act both strategically as well as tactically:

- **Tactical response – sell high and make your existing proposition more aggressive.** Your sales people must be able to interact credibly with top management. If they are only product-centric sales people, the CXO level guys won't want to meet them. Lets say you have those two products, Retail Branch Automation and Mobile-banking, but Retail Branch Automation still accounts for 90% of revenue. You need to keep that engine firing on all cylinders. So you have to quickly find out which Banks are doubling down on their physical branches; these are the ones that will invest big in the latest Retail Branch Automation technology. The managers in charge of physical branches will *say* that the Bank is totally committed to physical branches; this will echo the public message in the media. The CXO folks will also keep to this message with a sales guy who they don't trust; but they might reveal something in conversation with a CXO credible sales guy who they trust and have genuine conversations with.

- **Strategic response – align your company to the emerging reality.** You need to "skate to where the puck is heading" and become a genuine partner for your customers. This is the subject of the next chapter.

> You are here – First of Four Strategy Chapters.

  o **What you learned** – how to move to where the puck is really headed during disruptive times (despite being told that, "it's business as usual").

  o **What is coming next** – how to genuinely partner with big companies.

Sales is Dead, Long Live Partnerships

The word "partner" belongs with innovative, leading edge and other corporate-speak filler words that have become de-based from over-use.

Used by vendors, "partner" means, "pay enough to enable my high margins and renew agreements without question so that my Customer Acquisition Cost (CAC) metrics look good". In short:

> "Don't commoditize me".

Customers want to commoditize vendors. That is their job. By commoditizing vendors they reduce costs. Customers also like having partners, but when customers use that word they mean:

> "Skin in the game".

You need to offer three things to prove that you have skin in the game and thereby earn your right to treated like a partner:

1. **Pricing based significantly on business outcome.** If you are taking a risk in the transactional model, customers will respect your expectation to share in the upside. Licensing software by usage is not shared risk, because the vendor doesn't care about the customer's business outcome. This must be a negotiation between partners around shared risk and reward; the customer also has to put skin in the game (thus the word "significantly" which does not mean "totally").

2. **Proactive innovation.** You have skin in the game if you have invested ahead of the customer need. When the customer's need catches up with your innovation, they will recognize your investment in that innovation as your skin in the game that entitles you to be seen as a partner. The incumbent vendors can ask

customers what they want. To break into that market, you need to anticipate what they will want and invest in that innovation. This is not a one-time event; you need to be continuously figuring out what your customers will want in the future. This book teaches you how to use your sales team as "market sensors" to achieve this objective.

3. **Bring something else to the table**. We are moving to the next phase of Cloud. In the first phase, Cloud was about reducing data center costs. In the next phase, Cloud based solutions need to bring something else to the table that they have created in the cloud. The something else could be consumers or data or vendors that add to your customer's delivery capability. This is how you build a moat around your innovation, so that a fast follower cannot simply copy your innovation.

Becoming a partner with your customer is the only sustainable way to avoid:

> "The creeping rust of commoditization".

When you are entering a red ocean market (a market with a lot of entrenched vendors that is red because it is full of sharks and blood), you have the option of being the commoditizer. However, the relentless march of Moore's Law and other fundamental technological innovation means that no company can be the commoditizer for long. One commoditizer replaces another commoditizer. You can use commoditization to enter a market by being the lowest cost provider using some new wave of technology. However you have to sell your company before the next wave of commoditization hits the market.

At some point you need to add value, by anticipating needs and skating to where the puck is moving. You anticipate needs in "blue ocean markets" that do not officially exist, because these markets have not yet been blessed with a name by the analyst firms, tech journalists or VCs. What does exist is:

- A serious pain-point and

- Disruptive technology innovation that enables a solution for that pain-point.

> The beauty of a blue ocean market for startups is that it allows you to get established before the big vendors notice that there is a market.

Blue ocean markets are where you still have an opportunity to define, create and lead your own market category.

In blue ocean markets, you can bootstrap using modern tools and frameworks and the *"three projects to a product"* methodology:

- **Project # 1: Sell a purely custom solution, get paid and learn.** "Once means nothing."

- **Project # 2: Productize a bit, by turning specific features into configurable parameters.** "Twice is coincidence." Now you are ready to talk to everybody you can find who will tell you about their ideal future requirements.

- **Project # 3: Build a product that fits those ideal future requirements.** "Three times is a trend." Now you are ready to launch, hire sales people and grow.

Once you have built a product in a blue ocean market, you need to become a partner with your customers, by:

1. Anticipating their future needs.

2. Pricing that is significantly based on business outcomes.

3. Bringing something else to the table.

You are here – Second of Four Strategy Chapters.

- **What you learned** – How to genuinely partner with your customers.

- **What is coming next** – How to turn your secret sauce into Unfair Advantage.

Turn Secret Sauce Into Unfair Advantage

Fast Moving Consumer Goods (FMCG) companies are masters at avoiding commoditization. Think of Coca Cola selling sugared water at high prices or Gillette charging a premium for razor blades.

Coca Cola is worth around $182 billion and is one of Warren Buffet's core "forever" stocks.

> What is Coca Cola's secret sauce?

Coca Cola looks like a physical product-based company; consumers buy physical cans and bottles. Yet Coca Cola is as light in business model terms as Google, eBay or Facebook. Coca Cola is really a licensing business, like a software business. The way they have done licensing points the way to the future of the software business (and with "software eating the world", we are all software businesses with different skins).

Of course, Coca Cola is not revealing their

secret sauce. Could it be, shock horror, cocaine? The technical "secret" is probably totally banal. There may not be any secret at all. The secret is really a business model secret. The secret is how Coca Cola turned the concept of a secret ingredient into a massively scalable business with a huge competitive moat.

> Coca Cola's secret is business model innovation.

Coca Cola's innovation was to combine two strategies that are rarely combined:

1. Sold through channels (bottlers in their case).

And

2. Created a consumer brand.

Doing one is normal. Doing both was unusual when Coca Cola pioneered it (it is less unusual now that Coca Cola is such a well-known success story).

© Bernard Lunn, 2014

However that art of combining is more unusual in technology. It's like cooking. You have lots of components that go into a dish. You might even have a secret ingredient that defines it. Yet the whole is obviously more than the parts.

Consider the greatest entrepreneur the tech world has ever seen – Steve Jobs.

> When Steve Jobs innovated, he did so using multiple components.

At one level he did that to create a device like an iPod, iPhone and iPad with lots of components sourced from all over the world. However, if he had *only* created "insanely great devices", Apple's business would be more vulnerable to competitors like Samsung and Xiaomi. The reason that Apple is so valuable is that Steve Jobs combined great physical devices with digital services like iTunes and AppStore into a combination that still mints money long after he died. That is why Apple has massive amounts of Unfair Advantage (aka moat, aka competitive differentiator).

Think about how the software business is evolving through Past and Present to the Future:

1. **Past = Perpetual Licensing**. Close a sale and send a disk with the software. The software was the secret sauce by itself. This is like selling yeast to people who want bread; yeast is the active ingredient, but it is useless on its own.

2. **Present = SAAS**. You add hardware to deliver the software over the Internet. In cooking terms, you add water, salt, flour (commodity ingredients) to offer a loaf of bread.

3. **Future = Software Enabled Business Services**. This includes hardware – that is now the baseline. Software Enabled Business Services also

typically include, 24/7 guidance by experts *and* business process innovation *and* digital media that attracts customers to your customers *and* co-branding partnerships *and* proprietary data. To stretch the analogy, this is now a restaurant where bread is one item (given free while waiting for your appetizers).

As an example, think of a payment network such as Visa, Mastercard and Amex. These are Software Enabled Business Services. Yes, these payment networks have software at the core. Yes, they own the hardware servers that the software runs on. Yet they don't license that as a SAAS product to banks. They wrap it into other services to deliver transactions to consumers via Banks. That is how Visa, Mastercard and Amex turn their secret sauce into Unfair Advantage.

What Coca Cola, Apple, Visa, Mastecard and Amex

have in common is the art of the chef – to combine commodity ingredients into value.

You are here – Third of Four Strategy Chapters.

- o **What you learned** – how to combine your secret sauce with commodity ingredients to create Unfair Advantage.

- o **What is coming next** – how to lead your market by defining it.

How To Define & Lead Your Own Market

Market leadership starts with mindshare.

> First you win mindshare, then you win market share.

Winning the mindshare battle requires **intense clarity about your message.** If you can distill your message into a single word or phrase that defines your market, you have a big competitive advantage.

A business can do well by selling products and services into an existing market. To build a multi-billion $ business, you need to invent and then define and then lead your own market.

> You invent the market that you want to lead.

That is what Marc Benioff did with Salesforce.com. He invented the Cloud and then went on to lead it. Marc Benioff is a salesman. He is also a technologist, thinker, marketer and strategist, but at heart he is a thought-leadership salesman.

Of course it is not easy to create a new market category. Thousands of marketing professionals get paid millions of dollars to come up with cringe-inducing phrases and tag lines that last as long as snowballs in hell. Messaging clarity is so hard to get right because it has to be based on a very deep understanding of:

1. **Customer pain point**. This includes "where their puck is headed", the trends in their market, competitive pressures and emerging growth markets that they want to get into.

2. **Your Unfair Advantage**. This includes competitive differentiation and your secret sauce as defined in the last chapter.

If your message does not seem real, it does not stand a chance.

> Your message has to seem so real and obvious that, when people hear it, they assume that they have heard it before.

You need to sum up all that complexity, all the dynamics of customer pain-points and technology innovation into a single word or phrase. "Cloud" now means something in the technology business. It did not mean anything until Marc Benioff defined it.

> First Benioff won mindshare, then he won market share.

When you have mindshare, your competitors struggle to respond. I learnt this the hard way in the early days of the market for real-time application integration middleware, when technology such as Publish & Subscribe, real time messaging bus and Enterprise Application Integration was being adopted on a large scale in the first vertical niche market – financial trading rooms on Wall Street.

My company was the technical pioneer, with some great reference sites; in our view, we had invented the market. However when customers started to ask us whether we had an "Information Bus", a term invented by a rival company, things started to go wrong.

Neither of our possible responses was very effective:

- **"No, that is not what we call our technology, let me explain".** This did not work. Customers saw the Information Bus concept and automatically "got it". They did not want to waste time understanding some new concept. Coming up with an alternative message is doomed unless you catch things very early and you are very, very good at coming up with an alternative. Many companies, proudly sticking to the fact that they were the technical pioneers, refuse to acknowledge that a new market is emerging; this can lead to becoming totally irrelevant and fading away. Of course, most attempts at creating a new market category fail and should be ignored; deciding which ones are real takes judgment.

- **"Yes, we have an Information Bus and ours is better for the following reasons."** This will get you sales, but will automatically relegate you to the position of being a follower. You can build a good business as the number two or three vendor in the market and, if you time it right, you can sell out at the right time for a reasonable valuation. That is what happened to my company. However that is a far cry from being the market leader in a large market that you define, which was what happened to Teknekron, which was later renamed TIBCO (as in the The Information Bus Company). TIBCO became the leader in a large market that they defined and created $ billions in value.

Example # 1. The Information Bus

The Information Bus was so powerful as a message because it was:

- **Simple**. This does not mean "dumbing down". TIBCO was selling to a technically sophisticated audience.

- **Based on a genuine "aha moment"**. As related by Vivek Ranadive, TIBCO's founder, the moment came when he asked a software expert to describe why so many software projects failed. As a hardware engineer, Vivek could not understand why well-tested components could not simply plug into the system Bus. Why not do the same with software?

- **Visual**. TIBCO created a clear and simple diagram of the Information Bus that anybody could draw on a napkin and understand in a heartbeat.

- **Executed consistently**. Everybody stayed on message. Execution consistency is critical to messaging success. This did not mean salesmen had to become robotic parrots. TIBCO was good at thought-leadership selling. The concept was simply the start of a conversation that went into increasing levels of details as the company engaged in the sales process. Yet at every level they could come back to the simple Information Bus concept and diagram.

Think SAVE – Simple, Aha, Visual, Execution.

Marc Benioff did the same thing when he invented the Cloud.

Example # 2: From A Company You Have Not Heard Of

When you see the end result from a great company like TIBCO or Salesforce, it is like hearing about Isaac Newton discovering gravity after an apple lands on his head. Afterwards it is just no, duh, blindingly obvious.

It is clearly not that easy without the benefit of hindsight.

So to make it more real, here is another example from a company that you have never heard of (mostly because it was acquired early and its product was absorbed by the acquirer). The company was called

Information Laboratory and they had invented a product that could take in lots of data points and create a network graph so that you could spot patterns. Projected use cases included finding why electricity grids crash, mapping how human cells form into networks for biotech research, discovering key links in terrorist networks and finding monetizable patterns in social networks. Once you see that "everything is a network", the number of use cases multiply easily.

The product was brilliant and ahead of its time, but this was the "technology nuclear winter" in the aftermath of the Dot Com bubble bursting, so venture funding was out of the question. So we had to quickly hone in on one use case where we could get revenue. So we chose large-scale software systems, the old legacy systems with thousands of components. We could quickly discover the bad patterns in these "giant hairballs". Our pitch was simply, "the quickest route to diagnosing your big old software". This worked and we exited successfully via a trade sale to IBM. In a more healthy economy we would have stayed independent and eventually moved from this entry market (software) to other markets.

This is how Information Laboratory used SAVE:

- **Simple**. We fix old software quickly.

- **Aha**. The insight that "everything is a network" is banal today, but was less so in 2002.

- **Visual**. Our "knock your socks off" demo was when we imported some customer data and showed them precisely where their problem was, by showing them a visualization of their software as a network of components.

- **Execution**. We approached people with big legacy software and proved that our approach was quicker and cheaper than alternatives.

Thought-leadership sales guys must be involved with Messaging Creation

The best messages come from a synthesis of what you are hearing from the customers and an understanding of your unfair advantage. You cannot rush that process. If you force it and hire a lot of standard sales guys to deliver the message, it is unlikely to resonate in the market; then you will just blow a lot of capital on sales and marketing. Hiring external consultants to create your messaging is usually a mistake. At best, external consultants can act as facilitators, drawing out what is already known but hidden. Great messages cannot be forced out; they have to emerge from the market reality.

This is where thought-leadership sales guys help to create the message. Think of what Marc Benioff did. He was a sales guy who was always hearing from customers that they did not want to be bothered with implementing software on their hardware and that they wanted to pay on a per user per month basis. Thousands of sales people heard the same message. They took that message back to their managers who told them:

> "Don't be ridiculous. That would put all the risk on us. Also you have a big nut to crack this quarter, how on earth do you think you would crack that if we offered pay as you go licensing?"

Marc Benioff changed the industry because he decided to do something quite unusual – figure out how to give customers what they wanted. It is a fundamental mind-shift to treat your sales people as market sensors, the listening devices in your market. The industrial era sales model treats sales people as pitching machines, all mouth and no ears. In the digital era we have to get that balance right – we have two ears and one mouth. This is even more critical during times of great change, when you need an early warning system to tell you about the disruptive tsunami so that you can take action.

> Thought-leadership sales guys are critical to Messaging Execution

The E in SAVE[4] is Execution. Everybody has to stay on message. As Sales guys are the ones in the market talking to customers and partners, Sales guys are critical to executing on the messaging.

If the message does not resonate in the market (because it does not address a real need with a unique solution), the top performing sales guys will *not* stay on message. The A Team sales guys will *ignore messaging that does not work* and will talk about whatever resonates - and they *will* close the sale. Then they will leave your company and close sales for your competitor who has messaging that resonates. The C Team sales guys will *parrot the message that does not resonate* – and they *won't* close the sale. That is why it is better to have no message than a bad message.

---

[4] Simple Aha Visual Execution

Once the market confirms that the message resonates, you need to scale the execution, which means creating "talking points" that carry the message in different ways to different groups. For example, you might talk about it differently to the CFO, CMO, CIO and CEO and you might talk about it differently within different market segments (e.g. you use different talking points with Banks than with Consumer Goods companies).

Only a few firms can define, create and lead their own category/space. Many other firms can be niche players within that category/space. It is easier to be a follower than a leader, but this also requires disciplined messaging creation and execution.

You are here – The Final one of Four Strategy Chapters.

- o **What you learned** – how to lead your market by defining it.

- o **What is coming next** – we now move onto sales and "cut straight to the chase" by telling you how to find the key to a big complex sale at the intersection of secret sauce, customer pain and relationship.

Find The Moment Of Sales Truth

The "moment of sales truth" is that moment when you clinch a sale. Even in a 6 month long sales cycle with multiple stakeholders, there is a moment of sales truth when you can "see it in their eyes" that they are sold.

Thought-leadership sales guys find the moment of sales truth at the intersection of Secret Sauce, Customer Pain and Relationship Leverage.

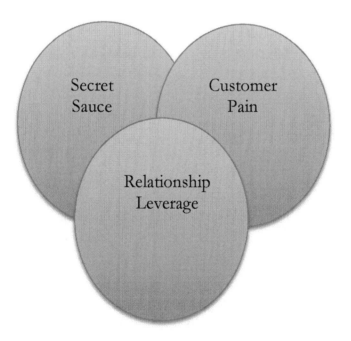

© Bernard Lunn, 2014

Your secret sauce is your competitive differentiator. It could be technology or process or people or data or business model or any combination of those. The product centric sales guys can talk about this "until the cows come home" – and until the customer yawns and looks at her watch.

You must connect that secret sauce to your customer's pain. That is what makes it solution selling. This requires a deep understanding of the market that you are selling into. You can hire folks from your customer base as sales people. For example, if you sell to Banks, you can hire an ex Banker with the right drive and personality and teach them about your product. These ex-customer sales guys will be able to talk about the issues that drive their market – and they will still be having those great conversations long after the sale was supposed to be closed.

You must have that conversation about how your secret sauce is key to solving your customer's pain *with the right people*. This requires a talent for building human relationships – in meeting rooms, on the golf course, in the coffee shop, in the restaurant or wherever humans like to hang out. That relationship building is a core competency of sales people. The great relationship sales guys will be able to call high and get meetings with the people that matter – and they will still be playing golf and spending the expenses budget long after the sale was supposed to be closed. These relationship sales guys won't win in today's market unless they also have a deep understanding of your secret sauce and the customer's pain.

That is why thought-leadership sales guys operate at the intersection of that venn diagram - your secret sauce *and* the customer's pain *and* your relationship leverage.

Thought-leadership sales guys move up and down the management hierarchy with ease. They are equally comfortable with a technophobic CFO and with the guy who can wear a goatee and an earing in a buttoned down corporation, because the CIO totally relies on what this techie influencer is saying.

> In the Internet age, these conversations happen too fast for the old sales process manuals.

In the slower-moving Before Internet sales world, the relationship sales guy had enough time to schedule meetings that connect your experts (either product experts or market domain experts) with your customer's middle managers.

This still happens, but only if the sales guy was there to nudge the buying process in your favor at that critical moment of truth. You need to intervene in real time to influence the conversation that is happening within your customer.

The relationship sales guy must be sharp enough on product and market issues to nudge the sale along in the right way when they find a precious moment with the key influencers, such as that technophobic CFO or that deep tech influencer.

Those two conversations will sound totally different. For example, imagine that you are selling a Governance, Risk and Compliance solution:

- The CFO conversation might be about the impact of what you are selling on the Stock Buy Back plan that the CEO recently announced. This conversation will be full of accounting terminology.

- The "deep tech influencer" conversation might be about the finer nuances of what real time means within the context of your product. This conversation will be full of technical jargon.

- To both of these conversations you drop in a reference to the headline disaster that just hit one of your customer's biggest competitors. Then you explain why your company has a solution that would have prevented that.

The sales guy will later have to bring in experts from your company to discuss those issues in depth, but if your sales guy is not comfortable and credible at both of those levels, your company will have *missed a critical nudge opportunity*. Done right, this nudge will lead to a conversation at an internal meeting (no vendors invited) that goes along these lines:

CEO: F<small>RED</small> (CFO), <small>HOW IS THE STOCK BUY BACK COMING ALONG</small>?

CFO (F<small>RED</small>): I <small>THINK WE MAY HAVE AN OPPORTUNITY TO MAKE IT BETTER THAN WE HAD PLANNED BY YYY</small> (CFO <small>LANGUAGE</small>) J<small>IM, CAN YOU COMMENT</small>?

CTO (J IM): Y ES, I HAVE BEEN BRIEFED BY MY TEAM ON THIS (MEANING THE GOATEE GUY FOUND HIM IN THE CORRIDOR AS HE WAS COMING INTO THE MEETING) AND, IF WE INVEST A BIT OF MONEY IN SOME XXX TECHNOLOGY (CTO LANGUAGE) THAT WE HAVE BEEN LOOKING AT, THEN WE CAN DO WHAT FRED IS TALKING ABOUT.

CEO; SOUNDS INTERESTING. FRED, PLEASE WORK WITH JIM TO COME UP WITH A PROPOSAL FOR NEXT WEEK'S MEETING.

Coming out of this meeting, your sales guy gets a call from the CTO. You now have the inside track on a deal that the CEO is highly motivated to sign off on. Your nudge paid off because the sales guy was able to operate at the intersection of that venn diagram. In two quick conversations, your sales guy:

- Explained the secret sauce to the goatee deep tech influencer (who then explained it to the CTO).

- Connected this to what she knew was top priority for the CFO using accounting language.

Your sales guy had this opportunity because she was a superb relationship sales person and tireless networker. So she was often "lucky enough" to be in the right place at the right time because she was *always out there*, meeting and networking. She had credibility at both the tech and accounting level, so both the tech influencer and the CFO where willing to listen.

You are here – First of Eight Sales Chapters.

- **What you learned** – how to find the key to every sale at the intersection of secret sauce, customer pain and relationship.

© Bernard Lunn, 2014

- **What is coming next** – how to sell when your customers are one step ahead of you thanks to the Internet.

Internet Changes Everything, Including Sales

The techniques for selling big deals to large companies (aka "enterprise sales") were created in the years when companies like IBM and Oracle were rising to prominence. These techniques worked very well. They were encoded into books, CRM systems, training courses, methodologies and the daily work of countless sales executives and sales managers. If you wanted to close complex, big-ticket enterprise deals you used these techniques. The encyclopedia sales person would recognize this world. It is all about CONTROL. You are taught to control the sale, to get that contract no matter what it took; it is a high testosterone game with a lot of sports analogies.

Then the Internet happened. This had two consequences:

1. **Buyers have control over information.** This is good news; the self-educating buyer dramatically reduces the cost of sale. The bad news is that we can no longer sell the old-fashioned way. The idea that we

could control the sale became ridiculous. We have to accept that we do not have control. So we have to learn how to have influence. That is what this book is about. It is not about how to sell. It is about how to *influence the buying process*. The difference is not a nuance. It is a fundamental mind shift.

2. **Risk shifted from Buyer to Seller.** This happened because licensing moved from perpetual to monthly subscriptions (or to transactional pricing based on business outcomes). The transformation of the software industry to the cloud and to Software As A Service (SAAS), moved risk from the buyer to the seller. If you sell a Perpetual License for $1m, the buyer has all the risk. Manipulating the buyer to close a deal was a rational response to this reality. In a SAAS model, the buyer can try it cheaply, but it costs vendors a lot if they "churn". Risk is reversed. This means that controlling your way to a bad sale, to a sale where you are not

meeting your customer's real business need, is a very expensive mistake for you. You have all the cost of sale and then after a few months the customer walks away and your Customer Acquisition Cost (CAC) metrics go pear-shaped.

Forget controlling the sale…

Herding cats does not work

Nudging a sale in your direction looks more like this…

First you win mindshare

© Bernard Lunn, 2014

Your interests are aligned with the right buyer. You both want to find out if there is a good fit. Your interests may not be aligned with 99% of the buyers, but they are perfectly aligned with 1% of the buyers. When you find the perfect 1% of prospects, your sale is easy, no manipulation is needed.

Mindshare to Marketshare is about discarding the macho notion that you can control the sales process in order to sell "ice cream to Eskimos". The Eskimos want hot chocolate and the Internet has helped them to find hot chocolate, so trying to sell them ice cream is an expensive exercise in futility. However the market for ice cream outside of Eskimos remains healthy!

You are here – Second of Eight Sales Chapters.

- **What you learned** – how to stop trying to control the sales process and focus on nudging the buy process in your direction.

- **What is coming next** – how to find that perfect 1% of buyers.

Reduce Customer Acquisition Cost

> "This is your CFO speaking. I am telling you what our investors are concerned about. Winning sales is not enough. We need to win them efficiently so that our CAC (Customer Acquisition Cost) is low enough."

"Easier said than done," you maybe thinking.

The right lead generation is key to a CAC cost that keeps your CFO and investors happy.

In ye olden days, most B2B leads came from outbound telemarketing or inbound via advertising or readers surrendering an email address when they downloaded a White Paper. After the Internet changed everything, a new breed of born-digital enterprise software ventures such as Dropbox, Evernote and Yammer pioneered new digital marketing techniques such as:

- **Freemium.** This is where you get users to try a free version and then convert some of them to a paid version.

- **Viral marketing.** This is where a user introduces the service to a friend/colleague because they want to communicate with their friend/colleague using the service.

- **AB Testing.** This tests different things that users are invited to click to engage further. For example, you may have a version with the Buy button in red and another one with the Buy button in green and you track which gets more response.

- **Social hacking.** This is the art and science of finding the line between extracting as much as you can about a user's social connections, without stepping too far over the line of privacy invasion and spammy behavior.

- **Search Engine Optimization (SEO) and Marketing (SEM).** How to be seen by Google in either the organic search or the paid search listings.

- **Content Marketing**. This is creating content that entices your target audience who then might be encouraged to engage with your service.

These are all Inbound marketing techniques. They bring us leads that we can close with an Inside Sales team. It seems like it is time to throw out the old and bring in the new. We can throw out all those old sales manuals and "let the product and the content do the selling". Let Inbound Marketing bring in the leads and let Freemium entice free users gradually into becoming paying customers.

Not so fast.

Ignoring the new digital techniques is not smart. Nor is it smart to use those techniques alone and ignore the wisdom of the past that created the software companies that dominate our landscape today. This book aims to marry the best of the old with the best of the new.

Many sales people tell you that the leads

generated by marketing are no good. This is an age-old debate (often acrimonious) between sales and marketing.

Marketing say:

> "You never follow up properly on our leads".

Sales respond:

> "If I spend all my time on your rubbish leads, I won't have time to sell".

Bad leads cost money. Many lead vendors sell on a cost per lead basis and many marketing departments are measured on this metric; so there is an incentive towards quantity rather than quality. Quantity in this case costs twice over – bad leads cost money to acquire and even more for sales people to "follow up" on.

The traditional leads funnel works reasonably

well in red ocean markets where the buyers are shopping for something specific. In the language of Search Engine Marketing, there is "Intent". This is very different in blue ocean markets where the solutions have not yet formed into products that sit within a defined market space. Hearing the screams of pain, does indicate that a market will form around any vendor who can fix that pain; but don't confuse that scream of pain with intent to purchase (which is what lead vendors sell), it is much earlier in the buying process. There is Pain, but there is no Intent, so Search Engine Marketing is useless.

In blue ocean markets, it is better to hire thought leadership sales people who proactively hunt for the few people in the few companies that will generate big results using a 4-step process that is like a funnel (the list gets shorter at each step):

1. **Pain analysis.** Is it likely that the pain you aim to solve is "keeping your prospect awake at night"? Rank your prospects by how much pain they have. The ones in screaming agony go to the top of your list.

2. **Competitor Lock-In analysis.** You don't want to obsess about competition, but you must rule out the targets where the competition has a lock on the account. For example, big old vendors will usually have something in their feature set that competes with your product, at least on paper. If you see a company that always buys from Vendor X, even their most shabby products, delete them from your list. It does not matter that you have convincing evidence that your product is in a different league, if it is clear that the target company won't pay any serious attention to this evidence. Your aim is to win business with the right CAC, not to be a dead hero.

3. **Leverage analysis.** You are looking for unfair advantage that you can leverage in this specific customer. This must have something to do with your technical secret sauce. Don't think that a Board level relationship is an unfair advantage; it is only table stakes. The sales skill is connecting the dots between a) the generic pain point that

all customers have and b) your technical secret sauce and c) the specific example of the generic pain point in the target enterprise account.

4. **Who are the "innovators with clout" in these accounts?** You need innovators who will pay attention to a startup pitch. Most people won't pay attention, because they are too deeply in the legacy box. However you can waste a lot of time with innovators who will moan to you about how stuck in the mud their employer is. That is worse than useless; it is a start-up killing time sink. You need innovators with clout. Usually this means they have delivered business value through innovation before, so the powers that be will pay attention when they come up with another innovation (the one based on your company).

You can do some of this as online research. Thanks to social media, we can do a lot more research like this than we used to. Not only is the buyer much more prepared before they meet the seller, the smart seller is also far more prepared than used to be the case. However, no matter how much research you do, "no theory withstands contact with the customer". Your aim when you get through the door is to validate or discard your theory about that customer; this is still part of the qualification process.

Within the context of this proactive lead generation approach, it is easier to see that the chance of a lead landing on your desk that happens to fit those criteria is vanishingly small. A good sales person will ignore all the leads that don't fit those criteria. Within that context, question the wisdom of using an inside sales team as a lead generation engine. Imagine a junior script-following inside sales persons getting that "unicorn" (an innovator with clout in exactly the right target account) on the phone; you just blew it with that unicorn.

Don't think Inbound *or* Outbound. It has to be both. It has to be Inbound *and* Outbound. Doing Inbound wrong will do more harm than good as it will generate bad leads that cost money to follow up on. Inbound lead generation only works if you follow three steps:

1. Define your Unfair Advantage

2. Create Messaging that leverages Unfair Advantage using S.A.V.E

3. Create content based on S.A.V.E.

Done right, Inbound will generate the same leads as the 4-step Outbound process. Having defined the ideal targets using the 4-step Outbound process, you can measure the quality of leads from your Inbound process. For example, if you say you want somebody in Global Sourcing in a FMCG Global 2000, any match from Inbound scores that lead very highly.

You are here – Third of Eight Sales Chapters.

- **What you learned** – how to get the balance of Inbound and Outbound right in order to reduce your Customer Acquisition Cost.

- **What is coming next** – How to test your Customer Hypothesis by doing the Social Media Dance.

Do The 4-Step Social Media Dance

The Lead Generation process described in the last chapter creates a Customer Hypothesis. This is your theory about why this prospect could become your ideal customer. Now is the time to test that Customer Hypothesis by doing the "social media dance."

Don't make selling more complicated than necessary. *Selling is just a conversation.* You know, where you use two ears and one mouth (listen 2x more than speak).

If you approach social media with that simple thought in mind, you cannot go far wrong. If you remember that it is a conversation you won't become one of those annoying bots that keep trying to interrupt conversations with their desperate blah, blah, blah.

Put a sign over your desk (or laptop, phone, tablet home screen) that says:

> It's the conversation, stupid!

Like any conversation, the opening moves between experienced buyers and sellers is where each is trying to figure out:

> "Should I invest any more time with this person?"

These opening moves now follow a *4-step social media dance*:

1. **Find somebody to connect you.** Use LinkedIn properly. Curate your network diligently. It does not matter which person that you connect with initially. Your target might be the CFO but you can still start in a totally different department via a buddy from college or an earlier job and then you network from there.

2. **Ping on a social network.** The ping follows whatever protocol is appropriate to the social network in question (writing on Wall, liking, retweeting, connection request etc).

3. **You check each other out online.** This is the first "should I spend any

time on this person" decision. For example you get a ping from a CRM vendor and don't respond because you are already committed to vendor X. Or it might be a new tool that complements vendor X for a problem that is relevant, so you do a bit of research by checking out the vendor and the sales person online.

4. **Some socially appropriate persistence by the seller.** This can include old-fashioned intrusive methods such as the telephone (now that time has shifted from phone to email, it is surprisingly easy to reach influential people by phone, because they welcome a relief from email). Most sales people impose limits on how many times they will follow-up, because it becomes counter-productive quite quickly. Don't delegate this to Inside Sales or outsource this. If you get that influential person on the phone you must be able to talk to them credibly.

> **You are here** – Fourth of Eight Sales Chapters.

© Bernard Lunn, 2014

- **What you learned** – How to test your Customer Hypothesis by doing the Social Media Dance.

- **What is coming next** – how to understand the buying process so that you can nudge it in your direction.

Nudge The Buy Process In Your Direction

The old school of sales taught you to *control* the *sales* process. Thought-leadership selling is about how you *nudge* the *buy* process in your direction.

> This is a cooperative process between buyer and seller; neither wants to waste time if the fit is not good.

Your goal is to become an enterprise-wide approved vendor. That is a ticket to 8 figures (tens of millions of $) per enterprise per year. Clearly, that takes time and you do it in steps but, if you are in the enterprise game, that is your mission. This chapter assumes that you are a "hunter" breaking into a new account, not a "farmer" who can wait for orders to come in.

The buy process typically has six steps:

1. **Senior management recognition that there is a problem to be solved.** This recognition usually evolves slowly

through conversations between multiple stakeholders. "Wait 'till you hear the screams" before you engage seriously; you must know that the pain is acute, that this is a heart transplant kind of problem, not a problem that an aspirin can solve. Start-ups have to get involved at this stage, even though on normal sales qualification criteria you should wait until there is a budget for an approved project. Incumbents can afford to wait, because they will always get invited to bid. Start-ups cannot afford that luxury. You have to be involved now, not only to get on a list of vendors; that is relatively simple. What you have to do now is influence the requirements. Great sales people can make the difference at this stage.

- <u>Your nudge opportunity</u>: **You have to find the "innovator with clout" and deliver the message that is the key to the sale.** The innovator with clout is the person who has the background to understand it when you say "the only way you can fix xxx (customer pain point) is with yyy (your technical advantage)". This is the intersection of the venn diagram (secret sauce, customer pain, relationship leverage) that is the key to the sale. The innovator with clout can then carry that message to stakeholders.

If you manage to insert your technical advantage as a requirement and make sure that enough stakeholders are aware how important it is, then you will be able to block the counter attack from the incumbent when they wake up to the fact that you are a threat. Note that all this critical selling is done well before the customer would be recognized as a "prospect" or even "suspect" in most sales methodologies. The key to doing this well is to cast your net very wide and qualify ruthlessly, a subject that we cover in the next chapter on having the courage, patience and smarts to "wait until you hear the screams". Think of this stage as planting seeds. Planting seeds should not take too long, most seeds won't make it but you certainly cannot hope to reap later if you don't seed at this stage. Note also that this is the time when you can build senior management relationships. As soon as you reach the next step, you will be interacting with more junior managers, whose job it is to manage vendors and "keep them in their place".

2. **Somebody is given the job of defining a solution.** This includes coming up with a list of potential vendors and a budget. This is where most "leads" come from and this is why experienced sales people are wary of these leads. Often the vendor list just needs a couple more names. Maybe they already have Incumbent Vendor A and Innovator Start-up B. They want to see what else is out there. They just need a list with say 3 or 5 vendors, because that's what their buying process requires. You can occasionally jump in at this stage and win, but the odds are against you. This is before a budget is allocated. It can take a long time for a budget to get allocated. The budget may never get allocated for many reasons – the

problem just goes away, they find a non-technical way to solve it, an incumbent vendor may show a just good enough solution based on an incremental module or version upgrade. This is where rookie salesmen are buried. The person that the rookie is talking to may be sincere or may be just getting some "suckers to the table" to fill out a list and make the buying process look good. Even if the person who is tasked with contacting the vendors is sincere, he or she may simply not know that another vendor has already tied up the deal. It is possible to "come from behind" and win in these situations, but the odds are stacked against you; so be cautious of leads that come from this stage of the buyer's process.

- Your nudge opportunity: **win over the inside-the-box manager.** You got into the game because you convinced the innovator with clout. To win the game you need to convince the manager with formal responsibility for this buying process. This person is an inside-the-box kind of manager. This type of manager has good relationships with incumbent vendors - your competition. This manager has seen you hanging out with the "innovator with clout" and is therefore suspicious of you. You have to win over this person and become an insider – or risk being a "woulda, coulda, shoulda" guy watching one of the usual vendors grab the contract.

3. **Formal demo**. Your company is now part of a formal vendor selection process. By this stage you are down to a short-list, typically with 2 to 3 vendors. This is when you have to prove what you have claimed. You will be giving a demo to a lot of people that you have not met before and may not meet again.

- Your nudge opportunity: **ensure that lots of people know that your secret sauce is essential to**

their recipe. You have done this demo far earlier, at the first step of the buy process as described above, to a few influential people. Now you need lots of people to see the demo. Your innovator with clout will have prepared the ground, but now you need to go into broadcast megaphone mode, to "shout it from the rooftops". This can be a generic demo; there is no cost to customize at this stage. The good news is that all the "buyer self-education tools" such as Freemium make this process of reaching lots of people in the enterprise much less expensive. Using online demos, Freemium and free trials, customers can self-educate before sales need to invest time. The buyer is investing time. The seller has the option of investing resources to use a human to give the demo. This is a qualification decision. Technical founders and technically driven sales people often confuse a demo with a training course, feeling the need to show every feature. This is where you need a great sales person working with a great sales support person. Remember what your mission is here. You have to create a enough stakeholders who tell their peers "I just saw xxx, we would be crazy to opt for a solution without xxx, it is the only way we can fix yyy (pain-point)".

4. **RFP**. If you get an RFP and you have not been through steps 1,2 & 3, you are almost certainly the designated "sucker at the table" that is there to fill out a list. Corporate purchasing policy may insist on a short-list of three. The company has already identified two vendors that they like; you have been brought in to "fill out the list". It is possible to come from behind as the "dark horse", but this is very rare.

- <u>Your nudge opportunity</u>: **formally insert your secret sauce into the recipe.** Now is when you describe that secret sauce in technically and functionally accurate language in a Proposal. If you have done your work earlier, the RFP will include your secret sauce; this is why the customer will take a risk on an unknown start-up. You have to do this in such way that the incumbents cannot easily "put a tick in the box". So don't just say "real time approval process" but be as precise as "approval process in less than 1 second on data from three external sources". This may become an addendum to the contract, so it must be accurate. Technical or product management folks must do this, sales people have too much motivation to exaggerate and many sales people are brilliant at communicating face to face but terrible at written communication.

5. **Proof of Concept or Paid Pilot**. This is when you *prove* that you have what you say you have. This is where you bake the cake and when it comes out of the oven, the customer prefers your cake because the secret sauce made it special (the remaining ingredients are standard). There are two ways to do this. One is the **Proof Of Concept**

(POC). This is a customized demo that you leave with them for some time. It is usually free. It is like a free trial, but you put in the effort to customize your product to their needs. The other way to do this is via a **Paid Pilot**. This gets used for real and the buyer pays – unlike a POC. This is a real sale, but it is a small investment by the buyer. As the vendor, you look at this as the first Land in a Land & Expand strategy. Tactically you may choose a Paid Pilot instead of a POC or do POC and then Paid Pilot. The decision is complex and situation-dependent. The prove phase is where you can leverage technology to reduce CAC. Tools that make auto discovery of requirements and facilitate quick customization can help lower CAC.

6. **Negotiation & contract.** This is the subject of a future chapter.

You are here – Fifth of Eight Sales Chapters.

- **What you learned** – how to understand the buying process so that you can nudge it in your direction

- **What is coming next** – how to stay focused on what really matters during the complex middle game of the buying process.

Focus By Imagining the Press Conference

The buying process can take a long time, a minimum of 3 months, usually 6 months and sometimes longer than 12 months. This is like being in the middle game of chess, when it gets horribly complex. When you are trying to prove product fit to an enterprise's requirements, there are so many variables to manage.

You keep focus by imagining the press conference.

Maybe you think that daydreaming sounds rather self-indulgent. Perhaps this is some new variant of the old "think positive" stuff?

Actually this is a very practical strategic selling tool. It is also a powerful visualization tool that athletes use.

Enterprise sales are complex and it is often really hard to see the wood for the trees; it is like the middle game in chess. Deep in the middle of the sales cycle, you are probably juggling internal politics, resource constraints, demo and proof of concept technical issues, pressure from partners, competitive moves and customer politics – and that's all before lunch!

You need something to keep you focused on what really matters. You need to know what is the one overriding motivation for your decision-maker. This is the story that your decision- maker will be announcing when the deal is done. She will present why her great initiative will have a big effect on one of the company's key strategic objectives and why she was smart enough to select the one vendor that was ideal for the project.

> Unless you know what this story is, you are shooting in the dark.

Even big, complex enterprise sales come down to the personal motivation of the ultimate decision-maker on your project. Customer politics can get in the way when the personal motivations of different managers are pulling in different directions. However if you know the personal motivation of the big boss (and if you are reasonably confident the big boss will stay in power long enough to get the deal signed) you cannot go far wrong. You can then focus on helping the boss align the pesky, politics-playing managers to the big objective.

To cut your way through the complexity of enterprise sales, you need to simplify. Select one person who is the key decision-maker. Understand what is important to that decision- maker. Select the one big reason why he/she wants to do this project. Select the one reason why he/she will announce your company as the right vendor.

There is tremendous power in keeping the focus to one. Find:

- **One decision-maker**

- **One business-driver**

- **One vendor selection-driver.**

When you see multiple answers, keep drilling and imagine that press conference. The CXO will only have one minute to describe the vendor and why he/she chose you; so there cannot be lots of reasons.

Imagine yourself in the buying shoes.

Remember when you have had to make an important decision and how you finally made up your mind. What you will usually find is that it was one simple reason and everything else was incidental. It was probably not a feature that hooked you; the anti-lock brakes on the BMW are good, but is that why you want to buy a BMW?

Even more powerful is the realization that there is often one precise moment when you win or lose a deal, even if the whole sales cycle is 6 months or more. This is the "moment of sales truth" when "you can see it in their eyes". Everything before that is preparation to sell and everything after that is managing the process to closure. Think about decisions you have made and how you made them. There might have been lots of research to get you to a certain point and then a key point when in your mind you think "this is it". Then you may still spend lots of checking to make sure you are doing the right thing, but you want the answer to be positive.

> After you have made the emotional decision to buy,

> you are looking for verification not problems.

Selling is a people game where intuition is valuable. You will know when somebody is convinced. It is less about what they say, but how they say it, the expression in their eyes, their tone of voice and their body language. No, that will not fit into a CRM system but that is a criticism of CRM systems, not a criticism of the value of intuition.

In some sales, you may not be there when that this moment of sales truth happens. This is not ideal, but it is the reality in many enterprise sales. At the crucial moment of decision, your decision-maker is probably sitting with the one manager that he/she holds accountable for this decision (the "recommendation-manager"). Again, there is one key recommendation-manager, although lots of other managers may be involved in the research and diligence stages. Although you may not be there at that critical moment, you must have a very close relationship with the manager who is doing the briefing and you and he/she must have total alignment on the key objectives.

> In long sales cycles, take time to imagine the press conference. Use this to get clarity on the "key ones" – one decision-maker, one business driver and one vendor selection driver.

Athletes do this kind of visualization. You can see downhill ski racers with their eyes shut before leaping out of the starting gate, their hands tracing the path they will take, their mind going over every bump and corner to the finishing line. It is hard to understand theoretically how this kind of visualization works, but the empirical evidence from athletes is clear that it does work.

> Imagining The Press Conference is also a great qualification discipline.

Great sales people know that qualification is a process. You do it every day, not just once at some point prescribed in a sales methodology handbook. Great sales people do this because they understand that sunk cost means nothing. It does not matter if you have sunk 6 months and lots of company resources into a sale; that has no bearing on whether or not it will close. Circumstances can change. Or you may have misjudged it earlier. If you cannot visualize that Press Conference, it may be time to pull the plug.

You are here – Six of Eight Sales Chapters.

- **What you learned** – how to stay focused on what really matters during the complex middle game of the buy process.

- **What is coming next** – how to qualify continuously and to wait until the customer's need is intense before committing serious resources.

Always Be Qualifying – Listen For Screams

The old sales adage is "always be closing". This confuses rookie sales people, because they think of closing as something that you only do at the end. Another way to think about this is "always be qualifying". The things you close before the final close are really ways to qualify.

Traditional sales methodologies treat qualification as a one-time event:

- Budget; tick.

- Need; tick.

- Decision-maker; tick.

That implies a linear process like an assembly line in a factory. Of course the real world is not like that, so you have to re-qualify all the time. This is even more true in the Internet age, when buyers self-educate online and appear fully qualified at the bottom of what we used to call a funnel and when the "innovator with clout" is that dude with a ponytail and sandals in the coffee shop.

As a sales leader, I love learning from the winners on a team. What is that consistent target-crusher doing right and can I teach this to the other guys? For a while I was confused by one of my best performers. He was, by most visible metrics, the worst salesman. His presentations were rambling. His writing style would have given my English teacher apoplexy. He came in late, left early and had long, expensive lunches.

I was really interested to find out what he did well. I do not believe in luck being a contributor on any consistent basis. So he must have been doing *something* really, really well, because he was doing everything that was visible very badly.

I discovered that what he was doing very well was qualifying his prospects with great care and discipline. We all know that is what we should do, but very, very few sales people do it at all well. We think that sales must be all about hard work, persistence, determination and all those other good Protestant work ethics. So we drive relentlessly on, calling that prospect for the umpteenth time.

This guy waited until he could see that the customer's need was intense.

> He waited 'till he could
> hear the screams.

He then looked for something to indicate that we had an edge in the deal, some unfair advantage.

His laziness was a bit of an act. In reality he was a tireless networker. That is what all those long, expensive lunches were about. However he worked to create a sense of equality and respect with his customers. Sales people are usually too used to getting on their knees to that all-powerful buyer with the big budget. So the buyer does not respect the salesman and will ignore five of his calls in the certain knowledge that he will get another one.

Yes, it is a bit of a power game. This power game is easy if you work for the dominant vendor in the market. The power game is hardest to play when you are an unknown start-up, when times are tough and you are behind in your revenue targets.

We were in that position when a small Hedge Fund came on the horizon as a prospect for our real time trading support system. This was 1991 and Hedge Funds were not on our target list at that time, few people even knew what they were. The customer certainly seemed smaller than we were used to selling to. So the salesman told the prospect that we were not interested in their business. This put the prospect in a position of selling to us. "Sure we are small now, but we are growing fast and we need this system urgently and we have plenty of money for IT". The screams were loud and clear and we closed the deal in record time and they became a good customer (and the Hedge Fund became one of the stars in this industry).

One way of checking for urgency is how much effort the prospect puts into the relationship.

> You need to see some equality of effort.

- If you call five times before the prospect returns your call, then that is

> not equality of effort.

> - If you send reams of information and give multiple presentations but the prospect won't fill in a detailed requirements questionnaire, then that is not equality of effort.

With every call you want the prospect to *do* something. If this does not happen then the screams are not loud enough and you should move onto your next opportunity.

You have to cast a very wide net in order to qualify your prospects properly. Otherwise you will catch a couple of tiny fish in your net and mistake them for tuna! If you cast your net wide enough you will find deals where the customer's need is urgent and your company has some specific edge in the deal.

> What really kills weak sales people is when a deal is going great, but circumstances change and the deal is now dead in the water. They did everything right, but the deal is dead.

Weak sales people don't want to see this, because it is too painful. That is when management has to make a painful decision to pull the plug on that sale.

Great sales people will also not be reluctant to say something like "we set this whole POC up the wrong way, we have to start all over again". If they see that the POC is not addressing the one thing that the CXO will mention in the Press Conference, they will be right. This makes them hugely unpopular internally, but it is better than losing the sale. The great sales people have the credibility from their sales track record to pull this off.

Great sales people are always visualizing that press conference and thinking about the "key ones" (one decision-maker, one business-driver and one selection-driver) and if it is not crystal clear today they will pull the plug even if it was crystal clear yesterday.

You are here – Seven of Eight Sales Chapters.

- **What you learned** – how to qualify continuously and to wait until the customer's need is intense before committing serious resources.

- **What is coming next** – how to close, get ink on the contract (yes, that comes at the end).

Closing - Forget Chess & Play Poker

I have used the analogy that enterprise sales is like chess with a beginning (get leads), middle (prove fit to requirements) and end (close the contract). In the closing phase, the game becomes more like poker where, as James Bond says[5]:

> "You don't play your cards, you play the person sitting opposite you".

"Closers" are rightly prized. Weak closers "snatch defeat from the jaws of victory". They give up a great technical/functional advantage to let a strong closer from a competitor snatch the deal.

There are so many books, courses, seminars and theories about closing and negotiation. Much of it "does not stick", because in the heat of the moment you need to make instant

---

[5] For Bond fans, this is in Casino Royale (the 2.0 version)

decisions. This is where experience and an aptitude for negotiating count.

However one way for negotiation tips to stick in the mind is to relate them as stories, particularly stories where somebody screwed up really badly or did something clever to gain advantage in a difficult situation. These are the Negotiation Ninja Says tales.

> Negotiation Ninja Says
> "Don't throw away the cards that have no value to you".

As a sales rookie I was reviewing the key issues before a major contract negotiation with my boss. We made a list of a) showstopper issues and b) "not a big issue for us" clauses. During the meeting one of the "not a big issue for us" items came up. My boss said;

> "Hmm, that is difficult. Do you mind if my

> colleague and I step out of the meeting to discuss this?"

I walked out thinking WTF; why make so much fuss about a clause that did not matter to us? When we were alone, my boss said:

> "So what do you think will happen in the cricket today?"

We spent 10 minutes talking about cricket. The idea was simply to make them sweat about a point that we were willing to concede, so that we could trade it for something that we wanted.

Negotiation Ninja Says

> "Test how nervous they are with something silly".

A few days before signing a deal, we were deep in the legal weeds. We were a tiny startup being acquired by a behemoth. We had a lot at stake, so we were nervous. There was a ridiculous amount of legal Due Diligence stuff. One question was:

> "Have you told your spouses about this deal and are they in agreement?"

This must have come from some earlier deal where a spouse had created a post-acquisition legal problem. In our case, our spouses just wanted us to close the deal so that we could pay bills and take a holiday. My partner said:

> "Actually we might have a problem there. I have not told my wife about this deal".

He was not trying to be clever, he was just tired and cranky and wanted some fun. Even though this was on a conference call, the tension on their side was obvious. The message was clear – the buyer was just as tense as we were, they wanted this deal to close as badly as we did.

In hindsight, we should have done this testing of their nerves a *bit* earlier. Not *too much* earlier when everybody is calm (because less is at stake at that stage) but *early enough* that it could be used to gain some negotiating leverage. The frayed nerves, the raised voices and the table-thumping, are all good signs that a deal is closing. You know that *you* are stressed. Find low risk ways to test how much *they* are stressed, to see how much leverage you have.

<u>Negotiation Ninja Says:</u>

After high or lowballing, use the blind pig stare and offer a mint

I had given the prospective buyer our price. I was highballing, had set a high price. He just looked at me. Did not say anything. Gave me no reaction at all. Just kept on looking at me. I call this the "blind pig stare". This made me nervous. The inner "monkey mind" was saying,

> "OMG, I blew it! I set the price too high".

The temptation to fill the silence was intense. The temptation was to say something like "it's all negotiable of course". I was not a rookie at that stage. I took a deep breath. I took out a mint and offered him one. Normal politeness made him say "thanks". The tension was broken, we started talking, found common ground and closed a deal.

Negotiation Ninja Says:

> "On the signing day, don't blow it by talking about anything more substantive than the weather.

It was signing day, scheduled for 9am.

There was nothing more to do, just go there and sign. The two bound documents were in front of us. I said something that prompted the buyer to ask me a question. I did not have an immediate response, because I needed to check with somebody. He said:

> "Let's reschedule signing to 9am tomorrow".

Later that day something happened that was totally "out of left field", beyond either of our control. The deal was not signed the next day. In fact, it never got signed. The moral – on signing day never talk about anything more substantive than the weather.

Negotiation Ninja Says:

Find somebody to be the bad guy.

Deals *can* fall apart on price. Despite all the kumbaya win/win negotiation talk, price is still one thing where the buyer wants low and the seller wants high. Sometimes you just have to dig in your heels and say no, to walk away from the negotiation. That bruises the relationship. Somebody on the team has to be the bad guy. That usually falls down to a VP Sales type person. You want the sales executive to maintain a warm relationship and you want the CEO/Founder to do the same. You are all agreed on the strategy and the risks of losing the deal, the only question is who will be the bad guy? This is tougher for young startups with a flat management structure. Make sure that any VP Sales you hire understands that occasionally being that bad guy is part of the job description.

Negotiation Ninja Says:

Once you start a bluff, any sign of weakness blows the whole deal.

The company was one week away from not making payroll. There was one mega deal in negotiation. We had set a high price. In negotiations, the Founder/CEO refused to budge one inch. I knew what was at stake and knew that giving say a 20% discount (on license fees which were 100% gross margin) would have enabled the company to survive. When he was asked why he refused to budge he responded:

> "If I had shown the slightest sign of weakness, the deal would not have closed. They had to see us as the best, most powerful vendor in the market or they would have got nervous about our ability to survive".

The deal closed and the company went on to great fame and fortune. This is poker in its purest form. Once after that, with similarly high stakes, I have had to take the same stance. It worked. It does not always work; but what definitely does not work, the sign of a weak poker player, is starting off betting high, acting super confident, then later in the same hand pulling back and "going all wobbly".

The Internet has changed everything – except closing; those skills are timeless.

> **You are here** – The last of Eight Sales Chapters.

- o **What you learned** – how to close, get the right terms and get ink on the contract.

- o **What is coming next** – now we move onto management, starting with how to manage thought-leadership sales guys more like creative people than robots.

Don't Tell Picasso To Paint By Numbers

> Many entrepreneurs fail by not hiring sales people that fit the life-stage of the venture.

Don't rush to replace the passion and creativity of the founders – which got those critical and tough early deals – with too much process too soon. This is a chasm that many entrepreneurs fall into. At some stage you do have to replace the passion and creativity of the founder-led sales in order to build a scalable business, but if you rush that transition you end up destroying what made your company viable in the first place.

> Everybody wants process – for the other guy!

Developers want to see sales guys follow a process, so that they sell what can be delivered. Sales guys also want developers to follow a process, so that the customers they sell to get quality deliveries on time. Both tend to underestimate the amount of art versus science in the other person's job. That lack of respect can lead to toxic behavior that damages the business.

When you see how the really great developers are not just a bit more productive than the average, not just 2x more productive but 10x, you would be crazy to load process onto their creativity.

Working with armies of average developers requires lots of process, but that is usually the maintenance type of work that is sent offshore. It is all about where you are in the lifecycle. Early in the lifecycle, you want to give individual creativity full rein. It is often one hugely creative, talented and driven individual who creates the original prototype; think of Steve Wozniak at Apple. Creating works of art, literature or music is not a team sport, nor can you tell Picasso to paint by numbers. A bit later you have some light processes for small teams – that is what Agile is all about. These are teams that work so closely together that "they can finish each other's sentences" and each individual is given a lot of creative freedom. In the latter stages it is all about metrics and scalable, repeatable processes.

> Be careful as you make the transition from artisan to factory worker.

By the time the product is a market leader in a big mature market, the sales team needs lots of process. You can visit the sales teams of companies like Oracle and IBM to find out how to do this well.

> To bring a new product to market, you need to unleash the creative drive of a few great thought-leadership sales people.

Enterprise software is complex. A simple concept such as Information Bus is just the enabler for productive conversations that delve into greater detail on the value proposition and technology. It takes years for a concept like Information Bus to become fully realized in the market and in those years you need thought-leadership sales guys who don't expect all marketing material to be delivered in a neat package. Thought-leadership sales guys are comfortable with the uncertainty of refining materials on the fly (those final adjustments in the taxi on route to a meeting and the post meeting debrief where you change a message that did not resonate).

The 20th century industrial era sales organization chart looks like this:

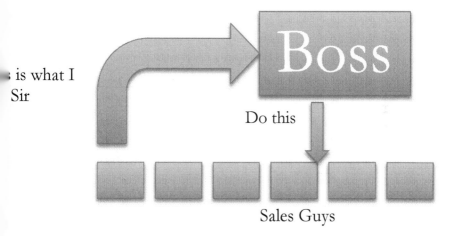

CRM systems are designed to help the boss control the sales guys. This is the world of hierarchy.

The 21st century digital era sales organization moves to a networked wirearchy, with the sales guy at the hub of the network:

Everybody in the organization is there to support the sales guy

"What can we do to help you?"

Thought-leadership sales people can be your rainmakers, if you discard the organization mindset based on 20th century industrial era thinking. The 21st century information era approach treats sales people as core, in the same way that other rainmakers are treated. Think of thought-leadership sales guys like surgeons in a hospital. The surgeon has lots of support people, such as nurses and anesthetists; the hospital managers also know that their administrative processes are there to support the surgeons rather than the other way around. Or think of Hollywood where the actors and directors are the sun around which all the other people revolve.

> **You are here** – The first of Eight Management Chapters.

- **What you learned** – how to manage thought-leadership sales guys more like creative people than robots.

- **What is coming next** – how to hire the Sales A Team, the quota busters.

How To Hire The A Team Sales Guys

Here are 9 things to look for to find the A Team sales guys:

1. **Track record**. This is easy with sales guys, you can see how much they sold in past years; but don't make the mistake of being too metrics driven. Selling a hot product for a big brand in a booming market is relatively easy, compared to breaking into a new market for an unknown startup. Being too metrics driven can blind you to the other attributes.

2. **Passion.** Entrepreneurs talk about the need for passion, because passion is what sustains you through the tough times. Sales people are "mercenaries, not missionaries"; but that does not mean that they lack passion. Passion is what makes thought-leadership sales guys learn more every day, about the product, about their market and about people. They are learning machines because they love what they do.

3. **Integrity**. Here is a bit of timeless wisdom from Warren Buffet. He advises that, when hiring, look for brains, energy, and integrity; but if the people you find don't have integrity, the other two qualities will kill you. Sorry, there is no magic trick for spotting integrity. Sure, do background checks, but also be human and trust your instincts.

4. **Intelligence.** Winning Enterprise sales is complex. It requires intelligence to understand the nuances of the needs of a complex enterprise and how those needs relate to a rapidly evolving technology.

5. **Empathy**. The ability to relate to other people at a human level is essential to sales. This is not a technique; it is a human quality that is probably a mix of genetics and early childhood learning.

6. **Great questions**. The great sales guys are not looking for a job, they are looking for great products to sell. Do their questions to you reveal an

understanding of the dynamics of your market? Are they prepared, have they done their research? Are the questions boilerplate or specific to what you do? What they ask in an interview will indicate what they will ask on a sales call; which segues to point # 7.

7. **Listening.** Great sales people have two ears and one mouth. If you listen well (really attentively with great questions) the prospect will reveal the key driver for the sale; the rest is easy.

8. **Energy.** The road is long and hard, you need physical energy. Hire sportsmen who know how to endure pain to win and who know that discipline (e.g. in diet) matters.

9. **Ambition.** Call it drive if you like. Mix with passion. What is it that makes you bounce out of bed the next day after a crushing defeat?

That's your checklist. How do you make sure you get these A Team players?

1. **Invest your time.** Hiring is your most

important job. Take the time to interview a lot of candidates; cast a wide net. As a side benefit, interviewing a lot of smart people is a great way to learn more about your market. Spend a lot of face-to-face time with the candidates on your short list. Meet with references (note, meet, not just email or phone).

2. **Don't compromise to "fill a slot".** It may allow you to check that box, but it will create 10 more boxes to check if you get it wrong. Don't be afraid to delay until you get the best possible person.

3. **Use the three months onboarding wisely.** All that talk about taking your time can lead to analysis paralysis and speed is of the essence in the technology business. Most headhunters will give you a three-month money back guaranty and a three-month probation period in an offer is quite normal. You don't want to make a hiring mistake, but you have three months to spot if you have made a mistake and then course correct

without too high a cost.

4. **Build a win/win compensation plan.** That is, a win for the company and a win for the employee. This is hard to do right. Even good compensation plans get gamed, which is why Buffet's advice about integrity is so critical. Be generous... but also demanding.

5. **Poach from the competition.** This is a double win. You get sales people who know your market and you weaken your competition.

> **You are here** – The Second of Eight Management Chapters.

- **What you learned** – how to hire the Sales A Team, the quota busters.

- **What is coming next** – how to get the sales team performing at peak level in both IQ (brains) and EQ (human relationships).

The IQ & EQ Quadrant

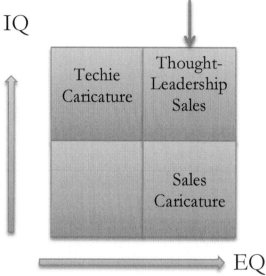

Caricatures run deep in many companies. The Techie Caricature is:

- Brilliant at coding (High IQ)
- Lousy at communicating with people (Low EQ).

The opposite is the Sales Caricature:

- Brilliant at relationships (High EQ)
- Shallow and not very bright (Low IQ).

© Bernard Lunn, 2014

Caricatures are inherited prejudices. We all have these inherited prejudices. Sometimes they have a kernel of truth. Sometimes they can even be funny. More often these inherited prejudices lead to toxic behaviors that damage the company.

Running an enterprise sales campaign during disruptive times is a complex business. You have to be bright (High IQ). To sell anything, you have to be able to relate well to other humans (High EQ). You cannot afford an either/or decision; you must have both.

> The IQ/EQ quadrant must inform your Human Capital strategy at both the recruiting and training level.

You cannot fundamentally change a person's IQ but you can make them smarter about your product and your market through training and "just in time intelligence" (see chapter on How To Turn The 80% Average Into 10% Stars).

However you may be able to change EQ[6].

> It is not enough to have EQ, you must know how to apply it.

Being able to relate to a person is the baseline skill. We all know brilliant (High IQ) people who are ineffective. Equally there are High EQ people who cannot translate that relationship building skill into results. Translating that baseline High EQ into influencing that person to buy is what selling is all about. That is "effective EQ". Influencing teams of very smart people to make big and complex decisions is what thought-leadership selling is all about – in the quadrant with High IQ *and* High EQ.

EQ used to be called "soft skills". This includes "parsing" non-verbal signals. I am deliberately using techie language, so that High IQ developers can relate. Think of this like Google parsing your search words

---

[6] Read Emotional Intelligence (Why it can matter more than IQ) by Daniel Goleman.

to come up with signals of your intent. As humans we parse non verbal signals (the arms crossed, the eyes wandering to the smartphone, the frown or smile etc). Unless we are Autistic, we all parse these signals. The question is whether we do this consciously or unconsciously. Most of us do it unconsciously. We may feel a negative emotion because a person with us is clearly bored or angry or in some way not showing us respect. People with High EQ can in the moment identify what they are seeing and what that means to us. Thought-leadership sales guys with both High IQ and High EQ can use the knowledge from those non verbal signals to steer the conversation in a way that nudges the buying process in your direction.

Your Talent goal is Effective EQ which is the combination of Conscious EQ + High IQ.

Most people can read body language (unless one is autistic). The body language affects how we feel, but we cannot consciously say "that is what I am reading and what it means".

Conscious EQ is the sales baseline. This is the ability to consciously read non-verbal skills. We understand that the crossed arms means we are hitting resistance and can tell the difference between the fake smile on the mouth and the genuine smile in the eyes.

Effective EQ is when you know exactly what to do to nudge a sale in your direction based on what the person is talking to is feeling and the intersection of secret sauce, customer pain and relationship leverage.

You are here – The Third of Eight Management Chapters.

- **What you learned** – how to get the sales team performing at peak level in both IQ (brains) and EQ (human relationships.

- **What is coming next** – how to use the sales team as market sensors that feed back into product and company strategy. This will develop Management EQ.

Use Your Sales Team As Market Sensors

> There are two core jobs in software; you either code it or you sell it.

In the great companies there is a culture that synthesizes the best of the coding world and the best of the sales world. In those great companies, both techies and hustlers respect each other and know that they depend on each other like mountain climbers roped together.

Sadly that kind of mutual respect culture is all too rare. For the first generation of enterprise software, the sales guys ruled the roost and they often abused that privilege. It is therefore no surprise that in the next generation, many technical founders sought to write the sales guys out of the script. This is the world of Dropbox, Evernote and Yammer, using digital marketing techniques to get sales.

The digital marketing world is 90% marketing and 10% sales and 90% of marketing is product.

> We now have digital quantitative feedback loop.

Marketing has become an engineering discipline. For example color choice is less about aesthetics and more about metrics – which color leads to more conversions?

Then you continuously refine the product to do whatever gets consumers to take the action that you want; this might be as simple as changing a color or as complex as a new feature. Analytics is all; or as the management mantra in Google puts it; "in God we trust, everybody else must bring data".

When a user engages online, that data is recorded in Marketing Automation.

> You use sales as market sensors in order to add a qualitative feedback loop.

These two feedback loops need to be in synch. In other words, the sales guys need to be in synch with product marketing. You need to hear what people are thinking and feeling about your product, to know what would entice them to buy more. When you find this out, you need to quickly integrate this into your product and your marketing; this has to be an agile feedback loop.

To create this agile feedback loop, you need humans who can understand the nuances of the businesses that you are selling to. This must include the nuances of the geographical territory and the trend line dynamics in the niche that you are focused on. These human "market sensors" also need to be credible inside your company, so that the voice of the customer is heard. In other words you need thought-leadership selling that is integrated into your product cycles.

> Your sales team is in the market sensing the next big market opportunity. The question is: are you listening to them?

You need to listen to your market at all stages of the venture, but particularly during these phase transitions:

- **When you are proving Product Fit To Market.** This is when you do things that don't scale. The most famous story that illustrates this is the AirBnB founders going door to door to get apartment owners to sign on to the service – and changing the product to fit what apartment owners wanted. In those early days you have to sell the early customers one on one no matter how small they are. Don't expect them to come to you and do what you expect. Go to them and ask them what they expect; ask them what would make them happily part with their money.

- **When you are knocking on the front door after your product has slipped in the backdoor.** Many consumerized ventures get into the enterprise via the back door, one click at a time using their product, often with a free version to get started ("Freemium"). They do this without any selling. Once they have a credible mass of paying customers, they knock on the front door to engage with their customers in what is a traditional sales process. To grow your share of budget you need at some stage to engage with the people who manage these enterprises. The alternative is to sell to an acquirer who can do this, but that is a very limited pool of acquirers. When you do start meeting these analog humans, you will be armed with a lot of data from your Marketing Automation (MA) system. This data is hugely valuable, but your job when you meet the big budget guys is to find out the data that is NOT coming from the MA and to set up a market-sensing process that augments your digital *quantitative* feedback loop with an analog *qualitative* feedback loop.

- **When the market shifts**. You may first see this as declining sales or some other metric related to Customer Acquisition Cost. The first instinct is to "give the sales team a sharp kick in the pants". That may be all that is needed. Or it may be that the sales team is acting like the canary in the coal mine that is alerting you to a shift in the market that you have to address at a more strategic level; disruption can sneak up on you.

- **When you are entering new geographic markets.** How do you adapt to different cultures, which definitely require adapting selling style, without losing the scalable, repeatable processes that you have built?

- **When you are entering the "bowling alley".** This is Crossing the Chasm speak for entering multiple niche markets as a step towards ubiquity and creating a general-purpose platform. You need to adapt to the needs of these niche markets in a way that makes you a native in those markets, but again you must do this without losing the scalable, repeatable processes that you have built.

- **When you move from founder led sales to a professional sales team.** This transition trips up many entrepreneurs. If you do the transition too late, you don't scale properly. If you do the transition too early, you lose the passion and creativity that made your venture viable in the first place.

- **When a market that you pioneered moves into hyper-growth.** This validation is hugely exciting, but you can lose the market that you pioneered by not ramping sales and marketing appropriate to the opportunity because you leave a window for a "fast follower" to jump through.

In all those situations, you need to deploy your "sales sensors".

> You need to create the analog qualitative feedback loop to complement your digital quantitative feedback loop.

That is how your company becomes a scalable learning organization and that is how your company prospers during these disruptive times when the dual tsunamis – digitization and globalization – are crashing down on your company at the same time as they are crashing down on your customers.

In the 20th Century, economy of physical scale was the key to growth. In the 21st Century, physical scale (such as retail branches and factories) integrated into vertical stacks can become a constraint on growth. More agile companies grow through controlling networks and data.

> In the 21st Century, the scale that matters is Scalable Learning.

You need to be constantly learning from your market, so that you can deliver the innovation that the market wants.

As an example, think of what would have happened if Marc Benioff's boss at Oracle had been listening intently and asking good questions.

> Listen intently to your sales guys and you will get inspiration for your next wave of innovation.

This is where you use the traditional sales review after winning and losing a deal. The analysis from winning a deal will usually result in positive reinforcement for the existing company strategy with possibly some tweaks to reinforce what worked so well in this sale.

The analysis from losing a sale is tougher. The sales guy will be feeling bruised and defensive. You need to overcome that by taking a point of view that a lost sale is ALWAYS a sales problem. It may ALSO be a product problem. For example if the customer bought from a competitor because they wanted XYZ (feature, price, service, whatever) the sales question is always "why did you not find that out earlier and therefore qualify out this prospect?"

Once you take out that defensiveness, the sales guys will be a wealth of market data. You don't have to wait until a deal is lost. If a sales guy qualifies out a deal based on them wanting XYZ (feature, price, service, whatever), that is good market intelligence that needs to be properly collated and mined to inform strategy.

You are here – Four of Eight Management Chapters.

- **What you learned** – how to use the sales team as market sensors that feed back into product and company strategy.

- **What is coming next** – the management problem created by the A Team "bring their own everything".

Managing Bring Your Own Everything

Thought-leadership selling is a creative act. This is essential in the early days of a venture when you are proving Product Fit To Market. To become a big company you will then need to create a repeatable process that scales. It is hard to do that without killing the creativity that got you to the Product Fit To Market phase.

Many startups stumble at the transition from founder-led sales (all passion and creativity) to professional sales (all process). Technology can help. This is described in the chapter on Climbing The Sales Effectiveness Capability Ladder.

There is one fundamental organizational mind-shift that needs to precede any technological implementation. Think about how hospitals support surgeons. The surgeon is the star. Everybody else is there to support the surgeon – anesthetists, nurses, billing etc. The same is true in sales. The technical experts, the domain experts, management, all of them are there to support the point person charged with bringing in the $$$.

If you want to see a fictional representation, watch James Bond movies where the folks at base are feeding real time intelligence to "our man on the ground".

There is never any doubt about who is the star.

Yet, some old-fashioned companies still act as if the folks "back at base" are the stars.

The great thought-leadership sales guys are in huge demand. They have their pick of great companies to work for. They are looking for great products to sell (tackling a big problem with a unique solution). They are also looking for companies that treat them like stars – or at least as respected professionals who can make a big difference to your business. One way they can spot if this is really true is how the company is adapting to "bring your own everything".

Bring Your Own Device (BYOD) is now a well understood management issue. What mobile device a salesman uses is not that tough an issue to manage now that HTML5 has matured to a level where it is perfectly acceptable for most business applications. Management does not care if a salesman uses an iPhone or an Android or a Windows phone, or anything else; if management does care…well run, don't walk from that opportunity. It's the app that matters, not the device.

> Management is now wrestling with "bring your own everything".

1. **Bring your own social networks.**
   You want to hire sales guys who "bring their own rolodex." The social networks, such as Facebook, LinkedIn, and Twitter, are their rolodexes. This relationship data is stored in the cloud and belongs to the individual. It is not corporate data in a CRM system that is used by the hired salesman while they are on the corporate payroll. There is a change in the individual relationship to their employer that is going on here. Data is

power and that data power is shifting to the individual. We can cheer the empowerment of the individual, while also recognizing that this creates a management challenge that is quite legitimate.

2. **Bring your own sales methodology.** In ye olden days, the company told sales people what sales methodology to use. It was part of "the way we do things around here". Onboarding included training in the company standard sales methodology. There are lots of these sales methodology and most of them are good. Famous ones are Miller Heiman, SPIN and Target Account Selling (TAS). However, will your startup be defined by your sales methodology? Or will you reject a sales star, a star that made the key sales for a competitor, because she prefers SPIN to your company standard? No, I did not think so.

3. **Bring your own sales productivity tools and apps.** This brings us back to mobile. It does not matter too much to the company whether a sales

guy uses iPhone, Android, Windows or Blackberry. However, what apps they use on that device has a bigger impact on management, because it relates to control over data and integration. The good sales guys will come in with their apps on phones and tablets hooked up to the networks and services they use in the cloud. They are onboard and productive on day one.

4. **Bring your own content.** The thought-leadership sales guys who are rainmakers for startups could be described as "bloggers who sell" or, if you prefer, "sales guys who blog". They will of course use the content created by the company, but when prospects can self-educate online before meeting anybody from the company, there has to be a reason why the prospect wants to meet that sales person (as opposed to meeting the CEO or CTO or CMO who is doing the company blogging). This is another management headache or tremendous opportunity depending on how you deal with it.

The mission that you are giving these sales guys is tough – break into new markets, win big new accounts and do it fast and do it big. You cannot also say "oh, and by the way, you also have to use all the systems, processes and tools we give you whether you like them or not". Imagine telling a sales guy who has used one methodology and tool set successfully for years that she must switch to your company standard. Do you want her to do that – or generate sales quickly, put you on the map in a new market and make $ millions for your company?

You are here – Five of Eight Management Chapters.

- **What you learned** – the management problem created by "bring your own everything".

- **What is coming next** – how to turn some of the 80% average sales guys into the 10% stars.

Turn The 80% Average Into 10% Stars

10% of your sales teams are the A Team stars who regularly make 120%+ of target. Managing them is simple. Pay their commissions promptly, give them all the support that they ask for and be generous to a fault on expenses. Make sure you know what makes them tick; the headhunters on retainer to your competitors know these guys.

10% will probably not make it in sales. They are your C Team players. Managing them is also simple. Fire them, so that you make room for A Team players. Do this as generously as possible – because selling is a tough job.

That's the easy part. The real job comes with the 80%, your B Team players.

> Turning a few of the B Team into A Team stars will have a big impact on your numbers.

Unlearning is harder than learning. Ask any person who learned a sport without official coaching. Like others, I learned tennis by just "hitting the ball around". I was reasonably effective at this, but to get to the next level I needed coaching and that is when I had to unlearn bad habits and that is far harder than learning good habits on an empty slate.

You will be hiring sales people with a track record and credibility in your market. So they may have learned good or bad habits; they will certainly not be an empty slate. Habits that were good in an earlier age may no longer be good habits today. That is where you use the talent matrix with Competent to Incompetent on one axis and Conscious to Unconscious on another axis:

- **Unconsciously Incompetent is a disaster**. You are bad at the skill and you don't even know that you are bad at this skill.

- **Consciously Incompetent is OK**. If you are a developer, you are conscious that you are weak in sales (and vice versa), so you seek help. This book helps technically oriented managers to understand enough about Sales to hire and manage well.

- **Unconsciously Competent is OK – until it is not.** This book is also designed for those who are so good at sales that they can "do it blindfolded" – until somebody moves the furniture around. That is what happened. The Internet moved the furniture around.

- **Consciously Competent is the magic quadrant.** This is what we should all be aspiring to. They are good and always figuring out how to get better. Consciously Competent people are not blindsided by change, because they are always re-evaluating whether what worked well in the past still works.

All sales people have been on sales training courses. Many have been on many different courses. Then they sell and many stop learning. This is how the whole education system works, so this is no surprise.

> What we need is a continuous learning via "just in time coaching".

This is like "teaching moments" with kids; you teach at the precise point in time when the knowledge is needed and the recipient is receptive to learning. This is what *good* sales managers do (the *bad* sales managers are simply report writers, administrators and political players).

Just-in-time coaching is quite simple. All you need is:

1. Great Sales Managers who coach by leading from the front (rather than sitting in a fancy office writing reports and playing politics).

2. A high Manager to Sales ratio so that those great Sales Managers can do their job properly.

From that description, it should be obvious why just-in-time coaching is actually quite hard. Those great sales managers are more rare than hen's teeth and that high Manager to Sales ratio will kill your CAC metrics. This is where we need some help from technology to make it scalable and efficient.

Nobody has yet built a "just in time coaching" system for sales, but the building blocks of mobile, social, cloud and big data are in place to do this.

To scale this productively, the "just in time coaching" must have a peer-to-peer element. Education studies have shown that students learn more from their peers than from their professors. Good sales people often tell you that they learn more from their colleagues than they do from their boss.

Unfortunately the monthly or weekly all hands sales team meetings are a lousy time for this type of knowledge transfer to take place. The manager needs to get the forecast updated, so this is not a good time to review details of what happened on a specific sales call. So this review is done one on one between the sales manager and the sale executive; no peers are involved and it is reviewing something that happened days or weeks earlier.

Sales managers who lead from the front by going to lots of sales calls with their sales team can provide this in real time but this is not scalable and so the CAC impact can be negative.

This is where technology can help. What we need is automated, peer based, just in time coaching systems that tell the B Team:

> "This is what the A Team guys have done in this situation."

There are lots of pieces to just in time coaching. One critical component is a knowledge base. This will be like a Frequently Asked Questions (FAQ) for complex sales. Here are some examples:

- **Q from B Team: When should I go to my contact's boss without**

his/her permission? Background. You have spent a long time building a relationship with somebody who always says the right thing, but the months roll by and nothing substantive happens. You know the boss's name but you want your contact to make the introduction, to "take you up the chain". Again, your contact makes lots of placatory noises, but it is not happening.

- **A from A Team: don't get in this mess in the first place, call high from the start.** The worst that can happen is that you learn quickly that there is no budget or that an incumbent has a lock-in. This is far better than taking a long time to learn the same thing. If you already started selling low, you have a problem. Do it and do it now. Don't warn your contact, he/she will only make it harder. Maybe use somebody in your management team or Board to make the call to the senior guy, but before you use your precious relationship capital, think about whether it is worth it for this account. There are only two outcomes a) you were wasting your time, the deal is not qualified b) they are seriously interested and you have a bridge to repair with your contact (if your contact is political player, he/she will be careful and respectful now that you have a relationship with the boss).

- **Q from B Team. When do you force something to a Yes or No binary decision?**

    o **A from A Team. Earlier than you intuitively feel comfortable with.** The motto is; "yes is ideal, no is manageable, maybe is the one thing that is impossible to manage". Whether it is investors or customers, a "maybe" closes off other options. This is where the old-fashioned sales motto "always be closing" comes from. Whether it is a time for a meeting or a signature on a contract, you are always looking for certainty. If it is no, move on. If you have lots of "maybes" you might not fill the top of the funnel properly because you hope that your maybes are for real. This is also where a conditional close works. If the maybe is based on a real issue you ask "if we could fix issue x, would you be willing to go ahead?"

- **Q from B Team. Should I use a Proof Of Concept (POC) or go straight to Paid Trial?**

    o **A from A Team. "The POC is the new demo and that's not good".** This means that too many vendors either a) spend far too much on POCs or b) skimp on the POCs so that they are not effective. Both are CAC killers. Weak sales people offer POCs far too early. It is free to the customer and looks good in the CRM metrics ("three prospects at POC stage"). Start-ups cannot win with skimpy POCs; you need the time to build something that proves to stakeholders that you have the secret sauce that their recipe demands. A Paid Pilot can also be called the first sale. It is a real sale with real benefits to the customer to real revenue to the vendor. By calling it a Paid Pilot, you signal a) your mission to be an enterprise-wide approved vendor (the Paid Pilot is a step in that direction) and b) you create a real dialogue/relationship with the stakeholder who is paying for the Paid Pilot by focusing on their ROI.

The Sales Knowledge base has to be tuned to each company, so that it is aligned to each company's market, product and sales process. (For example, one company may prefer POC to Paid Trial or vice versa).

More importantly, there needs to be:

1. **Hard data on what works.** This should be both from within your company and from other companies in your market. This Data Science is more effective than relying totally on the "intuition" of a great sales manager based on decades of experience. The great sales managers must be involved to make sure that the knowledge base is good.

2. **Ways of delivering the learning just in time.** This is where the new mobile-first sales productivity tools are a big enabler of change. If a sales person has just left a meeting and has entered some meeting notes on her mobile phone in a coffee shop after the meeting, the system has context

such as the stage in sales cycle and seniority and job role of the prospect.

3. **Ways to bring in peers just in time.** The expert system will come up with automated recommendations. However in the early days these may not be good enough and too many recommendations will lead to digital fatigue and they will be ignored. So the sales person needs to know who to call. It might be a domain expert, or a tech expert or her sales manager or a peer on the sales team. The system can automatically ping these people on their mobile phones to see who is available to advise right now.

4. **Digital exhaust to feed the knowledge base.** Mobile sales productivity systems know exactly what is happening. For example, these systems can know how many meetings we have had with that customer, how many emails they opened and so forth. This can start to answer questions such as:

- How many hours has this customer spent talking to us?

- Do they open emails from us and how quickly?

- Are they clicking through our slides during webinars or is their attention engaged elsewhere?

- How many emails did they send us?

If we can track that customer engagement through different stages of the sales process we can create the knowledge base that makes just in time coaching possible.

Just in time coaching enables an agile, emergent, adaptive sales process that empowers sales process. This is so different from the pre-Internet control-oriented mechanistic sales process.

You are here – Six of Eight Management Chapters.

- **What you learned** – how to turn some of the 80% average sales guys into the 10% stars.

- **What is coming next** – how to forecast when even your customers don't know what is going to happen.

Forecasting In A Disruptive World

Forecasting new business sales revenue is hard. As any sales manager will tell you, that is the ultimate "no, duh" statement. Yes forecasting is very hard.

The reason is obvious – the future is uncertain.

Sales revenue forecasting is also enormously important; just ask any CEO that has been hammered by their Board for missing their numbers. Forecasting drives so many critical decisions. Without good forecasts you cannot have a good relationship with investors and you cannot plan your business.

If the company is big and old, you have lots of data to guide your forecasts and errors become rounding errors. In startups the forecasting is also a lot tougher because there is a stepladder of forecasting difficulty:

- **Very Easy: add-on sales to existing accounts.** Start-up you don't have much of this and investors in mature companies are judging you by your success with the more difficult sales to new accounts.

- **Fairly Easy: new accounts within a geography and a niche where you have been selling for years.** This is the basic blocking and tackling of sales. It is not the breakthrough that investors and CXO folks want.

- **Hard: sales of a well-established product into a new geography or a new horizontal or vertical market.** These are the breakthrough deals that define value creation for your business. Translation, a few of these breakthrough deals will make your shareholders rich.

- **Really Hard: sales of a new product into a market that is not even well-defined yet.** These are the blue ocean markets that allow startups to get traction and scale. These are the game-changing deals that enable an IPO or trade sale or an analyst upgrade. This is a very tough forecasting challenge.

The law that I have observed in decades of sales management is:

> "The more value creation potential in a deal, the harder it is to forecast".

In a world where the disruption of digitization and globalization is hitting your customers, their behavior will change.

> During times of disruptive change, even big companies may find forecasting challenges similar to startups.

Forecasting recurring revenue contracts such as maintenance can be automated quite easily. You can apply standard assumptions about renewal and decay (how many will cancel) and the growth will be based on new contracts. This is simple data-driven forecasting.

> The forecasting problems all come from forecasting new contracts.

These are outside your direct control. You are extremely dependent on the judgment of your sales team. SaaS subscription models make new contracts less critical, but investors are still mostly looking for the new contracts (and churn) as the signals of success or failure.

You obviously want more sales. Perhaps even more:

> You want to know what is likely to happen. You want **accuracy**.

Attempts to automate new contract revenue forecasting often do more harm than good.

The standard approach is to apply closure rates to the sales funnel. The idea is to make assumptions about how many calls it takes to get meetings and how many meetings it takes to prepare a proposal and how many proposals it takes to get a contract. Then you can analyze the pipeline to say we have:

- 10 deals at 40% probability,

- 5 deals at 60%,

- 3 deals at 80% and

- 1 deal at 90%.

> Put all that in a spreadsheet and, hey presto, you have a revenue forecast – that is horribly misleading.

This approach appeals to engineers and accountants. It appears to be scientific. The problem is that it generates a false sense of confidence and is very susceptible to gaming as in "lets bump up the number of meetings until we get the desired result". It is a classic "garbage in, garbage out" problem.

It is also a static model. The assumptions built into those conversion rates maybe changing, but if they don't change in your forecasting model it will diverge badly from reality.

It is better to build a system around what good sales managers do in the real world. What they want to know from a sales guy is "will this deal close this quarter?" In the real world it is always binary – it either closes or does not close.

> 90% closure does not hit the revenue numbers and 2x 90% is still not worth any money.

Of course this leads to "sandbagging". The sales guy may have 2 deals that can close in the quarter. He will tell his manager that one will definitely close and keep the other one in reserve. If his "committed close" blows out, he hustles to close his back-up deal. If his main deal closes, he can either get his back-up deal in this quarter and be the star of the quarter and pick up some nice accelerator commissions, or push it into the next quarter and get ahead of the game.

Everybody sandbags right up the CEO providing "earnings guidance" to public market investors. Is this a problem? As one Board Director put it,

> "I love getting sandbagged, it means surprises are much more

> likely to be positive rather than negative".

Whatever system you put in place, it will be gamed. The trick is not to try and avoid gaming, because that runs against human nature. The trick is to get game theory working on your side by explicitly focusing on accuracy in two ways:

1. **Measure accuracy.** The old saw applies - you cannot manage what you don't measure. How accurate was salesman x in the past? Note that this is not the same as "did salesman X make target? The question is "at end Q2, salesman X forecast $1m for Q3. Now at end Q3, what was the actual result?"

2. **Reward accuracy.** Revenue is always rewarded, but with accuracy being so critical to the company, why don't we explicitly reward accuracy? This can be in "attaboy" gifts; rewarding accuracy with cash when a sales guy is way below target could be counterproductive. Yet they must be good gifts – such as the holiday in the

sun all expenses paid for top accuracy.

We do not measure and reward accuracy, because we are too focused on budgets and targets. These are only plans. Targets and budgets are snapshots of assumptions. What business leaders really need is a more dynamic model that answers the question "what will we do next quarter?" Accountants and spreadsheets can measure the difference between actual, forecast, budget and target and the gaps can be used to kick ass and revisit assumptions at budget time. But don't confuse that with the main objective of getting accuracy.

Many stakeholders are involved in the sales process and can add value in the forecasting process. During the regular sales review meetings all stakeholders should have a say. For example, the head of Customer Support may chime in with data about a nasty problem that Customer X is reporting that will not be easily fixed. That is likely to delay closing. It may also elevate that problem in the fix priority. Or, a salesman may say "POC for Prospect X starts next week", but the Head Of Professional Services who provides resources for POCs may say, "no, we cannot start next week". The key output from these meetings is a company view on where each prospect is in the sales Funnel (eg in POC, in contract negotiation, Proposal presented, first meeting).

However that must not replace a simple financial forecast from each sales executive by month. You record accuracy over time. Then you can apply simple metrics. For example:

- Sales Executive #1 has 90% accuracy,

    o She forecasts $1million for February

    o You record $900,000 in the Forecast for February.

- Sales Executive #2 has 50%accuracy,

    o She forecasts $1million for February

    o Your record $500,000 in the Forecast for February.

Note that the accuracy rating changes dynamically each month. If disruption is hitting your market, some sales people will be on top of this and their accuracy will stay good. Other sales people who are blind-sided by change will see a drop off in their accuracy ratings. By measuring accuracy ratings dynamically, the company accuracy does not suffer.

> By measuring accuracy we also get a good signal about the rate of disruption.

If accuracy is declining on an individual basis, then you have a coaching/training issue. If accuracy is declining on a company basis, then you have a strategic issue to address.

You are here – Seven of Eight Management Chapters.

- o **What you learned** – how to forecast when even your customers don't know what is going to happen.

- o **What is coming next** – how to create the people, process, technology ladder of excellence.

The Sales Capability Maturity Ladder

As always, one needs to aim for the top right quadrant:

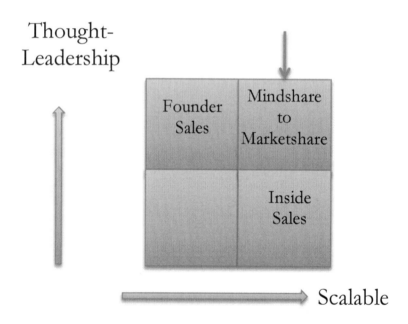

Founder Sales means all passion & creativity, which is the only way to win those early days.

Inside Sales means script-followers who can be managed on simple metrics.

To get into that top right quadrant, you need to climb the Sales Capability Maturity Ladder:

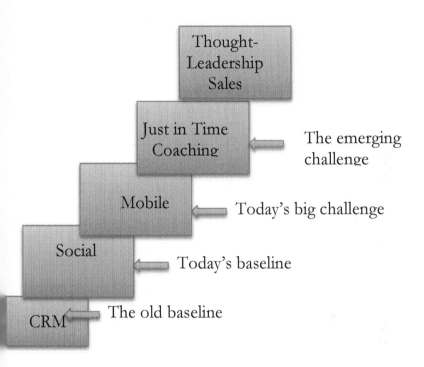

Step # 1. CRM is the old baseline. When your business scales beyond a couple of sales people, you cannot think about doing without a CRM system. Yet CRM is only a baseline. CRM is a great convenience for managers, but does it give front-line sales people an edge? CRM gave them an edge 30 years ago, when sales people moved from index cards to PC based contact managers – not today.

Step # 2. Social Media is today's baseline. Sales already use Social Media. Management's job is integrating that social media flow with the structured process in your CRM systems. Social Media is now as integrated into our lives as email and the telephone. If it is not also integrated with your CRM system your sales team will face the tough choice doing without social media or ignoring the CRM system. If you have not done this, you are behind the curve. The good news is you can leapfrog old social media using mobile.

Step # 3. Mobile is today's challenge. Outside sales spend most of their time out of the office, so they live on their mobile devices. If they are in the office too much, they are not doing their job. One pre-revenue metric that good sales managers track is face to face time. How much time are they spending face to face with customers? Everything else is preparation or follow-up, which is essential, but actual selling takes place face to face (or on the phone).

Today's Challenge is making everything Mobile friendly, to save time for outside sales people. There are mobile add-ons from CRM vendors and mobile-first ventures that can work with any CRM system. These mobile enablement systems take the lower rungs as inputs, meaning that CRM data and social data is integrated into the mobile workflow in order to deliver two benefits:

- **Reducing CRM admin work.** It should be possible to do reports in the elevator or coffee shop in between meetings.

- **Making it easier to set up meetings.** This is done via integration of things like maps and calendars on a mobile phone.

Neither of these are game-changers, but they do add productive hours and at scale that matters. However making workflow mobile-first sets the stage for a more strategic value at the next step of the ladder.

Step # 4: Just In Time Coaching.

Sales people do not work alone. This is where Mobile intersects with Data Science and becomes an enterprise story. The sales people are out there, meeting people in the market, but they are in touch with support teams "back at base".

The emerging challenge, is what I have described in the chapter on *"How To Turn The 80% Average Into 10% Stars"*. These are Insights that are delivered "context aware", so you only get what is relevant, and "just in time", so that the Insight is actionable right now. These Insights are delivered to your mobile device and use content from internal CRM and BI systems as well as social media and external business intelligence. These Insights can be delivered as content but can also be delivered by humans (what I call "just in time coaching").

Step # 5: Thought-Leadership Sales

The top of the Sales Effectiveness Maturity Ladder is when all the technology is implemented using best practice methodologies and training.

> **You are here** – The last of Eight Management Chapters.

- o **What you learned** – how to create the people, process and technology ladder of excellence.

- o **What is coming next** – the final summary chapter.

Sell To YOUR Ideal Customer

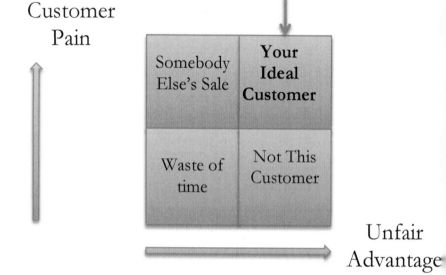

Somebody Else's Sale:
- You correctly identified a major pain point.
BUT
- You don't have an Unfair Advantage

Not This Customer:
- They love your product/service.
BUT
- It is not relevant to their Customer Pain A List

The Internet changes everything – including the traditional Sales Funnel:

- The ratio of Suspects to Prospects goes up dramatically. Rather than being 3x in the Before Internet Funnel, it is now more like 30x or even 300x. There is a huge Cloud of Suspects out there. You will never meet most of them; they will self-qualify themselves out based on what they read online

- The Prospect to Close ratio improves, because the Suspects qualify themselves out more ruthlessly than your sales team ever did. If you Qualify properly, you can afford to throw all your available resources to win a deal. You "throw everything at it". You don't count the cost. Yes, you can still lose some, but you won't lose them for lack of resources or budget. You will also only lose a very small number, so this does not kill your CAC metrics.

- Of course, if you don't qualify properly and apply the same expensive resources to every prospect, your Customer Acquisition Cost will go through the roof.

Your ideal customers are out there and your interests are 100% aligned with that ideal customer. You both want to find out if there is a good fit. Your interests not be aligned with 99% of the buyers, but they are perfectly aligned with 1% of the buyers. When you find the perfect 1% of prospects, your sale is easy; you do not need to control the sale, you only need to gently nudge it in your direction.

Printed in Great Britain
by Amazon.co.uk, Ltd.,
Marston Gate.